D0744634

PERCEPTION AND PERSONAL
IDENTITY

PERCEPTION
AND
PERSONAL
IDENTITY

Proceedings of the
1967 Oberlin Colloquium in Philosophy

EDITED BY
NORMAN S. CARE
AND
ROBERT H. GRIMM

The Press of
Case Western Reserve University
Cleveland / 1969

Preface

This volume is the Proceedings of the eighth annual Oberlin Colloquium in Philosophy (1967). The Colloquium is sponsored by the Department of Philosophy of Oberlin College to provide an opportunity for the presentation and close, extended discussion of new work in philosophy. The intention is, so far as possible, to restrict each Colloquium to a single general topic, or to a set of closely related topics. The 1967 Colloquium consisted of five sessions, three of which were symposia, and an invited group of philosophers took part in all. The papers that were presented are published here for the first time; from the symposia there are comments and replies in addition to the papers.

Richard H. Popkin's opening paper provides an historical account of the origins in sixteenth-century scepticism of the problems that occupy epistemology in the modern period of philosophy, several of which receive considerable attention in the symposia that follow. In "Thinking and Doing," Robert J. Fogelin develops an interpretation of Aristotle's remarks about the practical syllogism into an "outline for a theory of action," designed to provide an understanding of some basic features of act descriptions.

In the first symposium Fred I. Dretske argues for a certain application of the general point that perceptual reports indicate how a perceiver came to have only a small part of the information that such reports imply the perceiver possesses. Philip Hugly's comments are centered on whether or not the point Dretske argues for can indeed be construed as showing that traditional sceptical considerations are irrelevant to the validity of ordinary perceptual claims.

In the second symposium Roderick M. Chisholm discusses, and argues in support of, two theses of Bishop Butler: (1) that when we say of a *physical thing* existing at one time that it is identical with, or the same as, a physical thing existing at some other time, we are using the expression "the same as," or "identical with," in a "loose and popular sense"; but (2) that when we say of a *person* existing at one time that he is identical with, or the same as, a person existing at some other time, we are using "the same as," or "identical with," in a "strict and philosophical sense." Sydney S. Shoemaker agrees with Chisholm that there are differences between the identity of things and the identity of persons, but argues that these differences are not captured by saying that only the latter is identity in the "strict and philosophical sense."

In the final symposium Jaakko Hintikka claims that the logic of perception is a branch of modal logic, and argues for this in two ways: (1) by outlining the basic reasons why the logic of perception is susceptible to the same sort of treatment as other modal logics, and (2) by showing that the treatment of perceptual concepts as modal notions sheds new light on some classical issues in the philosophy of perception. In his comments Romane Clark accepts Hintikka's general contention, but objects to some details of his treatment of the substitutivity of identicals and existential generalization.

The authors for the Colloquium in 1967 came from eight universities: Popkin from the University of California at San Diego, Fogelin from Yale University, Dretske from the University of Wisconsin, Hugly from the University of Texas, Chisholm from Brown University, Shoemaker from Cornell University (he has since moved to the Rockefeller University), Hintikka from Stanford University and the University of Helsinki, and Clark from Duke University. The members of the Department of Philosophy of Oberlin College are indebted to the speakers for their contributions and to the other philosophers at the Colloquium for their participation. They also wish to thank Oberlin College for its continuing support of the Oberlin Colloquium in Philosophy.

N.S.C. and R.H.G.
for the Department of Philosophy
Oberlin College

Contents

Preface   v

RICHARD H. POPKIN
The Sceptical Origins of the
Modern Problem of Knowledge   3

ROBERT J. FOGELIN
Thinking and Doing   25

Symposium
FRED I. DRETSKE
Seeing and Justification   42
PHILIP HUGLY
Comments   53
FRED I. DRETSKE
Reply   71

Symposium
RODERICK M. CHISHOLM
The Loose and Popular and the
Strict and Philosophical Senses of
Identity   82
SYDNEY S. SHOEMAKER
Comments   107
RODERICK M. CHISHOLM
Reply   128

Symposium
JAAKKO HINTIKKA
On the Logic of Perception   140
ROMANE CLARK
Comments   174
JAAKKO HINTIKKA
Reply   188

PERCEPTION AND PERSONAL IDENTITY

The Sceptical Origins of the Modern Problem of Knowledge

RICHARD H. POPKIN

It seems to me that two of the main interpretations that have been offered to account for the occurrence of the problem of knowledge that dominated philosophy from Descartes down to at least the period of Hume and Kant are incorrect or inadequate. One of these interpretations is the one most forcefully presented in John Herman Randall's recent work, *The Career of Philosophy*, namely, that the occurrence of the problem of knowledge was due to the development of modern science, especially Galilean physics, and the attempt to interpret and understand the world revealed by the "new science" after Aristotelian epistemology had been rejected.[1] The other interpretation is the one that dominated German and Germanic histories of philosophy in the latter half of the nineteenth century, namely, the view that the problem of knowledge was due to the rejection of Scholasticism, and the attempts to replace it with rationalism and empiricism as thoroughgoing accounts of how knowledge occurs and of what is known.[2]

In contrast to these theories, my own view is that the sceptical crises of the sixteenth century posed the modern problem of knowledge and shaped its form, and that the types of answers to the problem offered during the seventeenth century were geared to meeting the sceptical problems that had been raised. This is not to say that the "new science" did not play an important role in the form that the answers took, and that the development of

[1]John Herman Randall, Jr., *The Career of Philosophy* (New York, 1962), Book III.

[2]See, for instance, Kuno Fischer's *Geschichte der neuren Philosophie* (Heidelberg, 1897–1910), esp. the volumes on Bacon and Descartes.

this science did not complicate the issues involved. (In fact, I think it could be well argued that certain of the epistemological components of the formulations then offered of the "new science," such as those involved in the primary-secondary quality theory, were themselves actually aspects of the new scepticism.) Similarly, the rejection of Scholasticism was definitely part of what was then going on. However, I would contend that, in terms of the epistemological issues involved, it was the scepticism of the sixteenth century that did raise certain problems in this context, and that it was this scepticism and the challenge it posed that led to the presentation of a series of responses that we now call "modern philosophy." These responses were attempts to solve or resolve these sceptical problems of knowledge.

What I am saying is not intended as an attempt to deny the obvious, namely, that there was a great deal of epistemological interest and concern during the Middle Ages, and that this interest and concern continued into the sixteenth century, and even took on new forms in the writings of the Spanish Scholastics. I am contending, however, that a very special kind of epistemological problem arose out of the monumental sceptical crisis produced by currents of the Renaissance and the Reformation, and that the effects of this crisis were put into a special form due to the revival of ancient Pyrrhonian scepticism during this period, and that the resulting presentations in turn constituted the very core of the problem of knowledge that Francis Bacon, René Descartes, and others were trying to resolve.

Several factors contributed to making up the peculiar characteristics of the sixteenth-century sceptical crisis. First of all, I should like to mention briefly some of those that played a role in casting doubt upon all of the previous achievements of the Scholastic world and upon the methods that had been employed there in attempting to reach true knowledge about the world.

The writings and the attitude of Erasmus and his associates seem to have been extremely influential in changing the whole intellectual atmosphere from one in which Scholastic methods and purported achievements could be taken seriously, to one in which these no longer appeared relevant to man's quest for knowledge. After Erasmus had finished ridiculing the Scholastics, their activities and their claims became trivial and futile for the sixteenth-century world (and later ones as well). Erasmus did not really undertake any sustained sceptical analysis of Scholasticism; instead he portrayed it in such a way that his intelligent contemporaries could no longer take it seriously and could no longer have any genuine confidence that such an approach to human knowledge would yield true and certain conclusions. The result of Erasmus' scathing attacks was to change the climate of opinion so that wise men of the time would reject all of the achievements and methods of the previous intellectual age, thereby creating a general rather than a specially philosophical scepticism.

The plethora of reports from the Voyages of Discovery further intensified doubts regarding purported knowledge of the world and ways of obtaining such knowledge. It was not merely the accumulation of new geographical facts and confrontations with radically different cultures that disturbed people's picture of the world, but more it was the interpretation of this new data. Amerigo Vespucci, who gave what was then the most popular report of the findings of the explorers, saw that the new information about the character of the New World, and of its inhabitants, showed that all previous pictures of the world were untrue, and that one could no longer rely upon the science and philosophy that had led to such a picture. Further, the new worlds, which seemed to function successfully without the moral, religious, political, or social institutions of Christian Europe, then posed a sceptical challenge to the Judeo-Christian and European knowledge claims about the nature and destiny of man. The Noble Savage, discovered by Columbus and extravagantly praised by Montaigne, posed a reason for doubting the ideology of the Western world. If people could actually live better, or even well, outside of Christendom, could one be so sure any longer of the truth and importance of the prevailing world view?

Another factor that helped create a general sceptical atmosphere was, I believe, the rise of interest in and concern with secret sources of true knowledge, such as magic and the cabala. The enormous role of these esoteric movements in undermining confidence in previous knowledge claims has, I think, been overlooked until quite recently. Figures like Johannes Reuchlin and Agrippa von Nettesheim (himself one of the founders of modern scepticism) had a great influence on the sixteenth-century world with their claims that the usual ways of gaining knowledge cannot succeed in finding the crucial truths about the world, and that only by employing methods other than the ordinary empirical and rational ones can one discover what the world is really like. The immense popularity of the hermetic magical works, rediscovered at the height of the Renaissance, of the Hebrew cabala imported from Spain, of the researches of the alchemists, the numerologists, and others, all indicate a general rejection of the normal paths to knowledge and a scepticism about the purported findings of previous scholars.[3]

Further, the humanist movement, with its emphasis on researches into the past rather than on Scholastic philosophical analyses of questions, contributed to changing the intellectual atmosphere and to casting doubt upon the knowledge claims of its predecessors. The rediscovery of the glories that were Greece and the grandeur that was Rome convinced many that the nature of the world had not been and was not going to be found through the methods of the Scholastic philosophies and scientists, but only by an entirely new approach, that of the humanistic scholars. The revolutonary recasting of the universities under the influence of Erasmus and his friends represented a total scepticism about previous intellectual enterprise.

These factors, Erasmus' anti-intellectualism and anti-Scholasticism, the interpretation of the Voyages of Exploration, the esoteric movements, and the humanist revival, all contributed greatly to creating an intellectual atmosphere in which the Scholastic world and its vaunted achievements could no longer be accepted, and in which its methods and results were doubted. A kind of generalized scepticism about usual knowledge claims was all pervasive. The massive structure of a previous intellectual world was eroded and nothing firm had replaced it.

Into such a world, filled with doubts and uncertainties, religious struggles injected an issue that was to strike to the very heart of human certainty and create a genuine sceptical crisis. The assurance one had in the Christian Revelation and the Chris-

---

[3]The recent studies by Frances Yates, *Giordano Bruno and the Hermetic Tradition* (Chicago, 1964) ; François Secret, *Le Zôhar chez les Kabbalistes Chrétiens de la Renaissance* (The Hague, 1964) ; and Charles Nauert, *Agrippa and the Crisis of Renaissance Thought* (Urbana, Ill., 1965), all indicate the great influence of the cabala and the hermetic writings on sixteenth-century thought. Nauert argues that Agrippa's scepticism in part derives from his occult theories.

tian world view was in part shaken by the impact of other religions. Judaism had, from the first century on, constituted a kind of challenge. If the very people to whom God had originally spoken, and among whom Jesus lived and died, rejected the Christian message, could one be sure it was true? Explanations had been offered from St. Paul's time onward to account for the Jewish rejection of Christianity, and massive efforts had been made from Roman times through to the Crusades and the Spanish Inquisition to end this challenge by force, forced conversion, economic pressure, and extermination. However, the problem became more acute with the movement of large numbers of educated and influential Jews into Europe from Spain and Portugal as the result of the ferocious persecutions in Iberia, and the revival of contact with and concern with Hebrew literature in the Renaissance and Reformation. Luther and the Jesuits were extremely concerned with the problem of why the Jews didn't convert. Bodin's dialogue, the *Heptaplomeres*,[4] seems to portray some of the ferment of the time, offering us a discussion among proponents of various religious views as to which is the true religion, and then having the Jew win the argument. The popularity of anti-Jewish tracts from Spain, like Pablo da Santa Maria's *Scrutiny of the Scriptures*,[5] also seems to reflect the challenge Christianity was undergoing on this score.

To a much lesser extent, there was a challenge from Islam. The Mohammedan claim that they had received a revelation that superseded the Christian one was of course troubling. Although this claim had not been taken seriously by the inhabitants of Christian Europe, the European world was pressed from Spain, to Central Europe, to the Near East, to North Africa, by believers in this post-Christian faith. And, in the sixteenth century, through the efforts of the Ottoman Turks, Europe was in military if not intellectual danger of becoming Moslem.

In addition to the challenges of faiths from the same revealed religious tradition, European Christendom was in the sixteenth century faced with the revival of paganism in its Greco-Roman

[4]Jean Bodin, *Heptaplomeres,* first published in 1841 and 1857. This work circulated widely in manuscript in the late sixteenth and early seventeenth centuries.

[5]Manuscripts of this work can be found all over Europe; it was printed in Rome in 1470.

forms and in the idealized versions of religions reported by the explorers. The humanists rediscovered the religions of antiquity, which held a genuine appeal for some. In the ethics of the Stoics and Epicureans they found better moral advice and teachings than in Christianity (or at least they tried to make the advice coequal). In America, Africa, and the Orient, they believed they had found better conduct among the Noble Savages, though these people were not guided by any special revelation, than in Christian Europe, with its constant wars, brutality, inhumanity, dishonesty, and gross immorality.

All of these matters could easily induce some doubt as to whether it was possible to gain true religious knowledge. Competing views and competing knowledge claims had bred scepticism in antiquity. The problem was pushed well beyond this initial stage, however, by the dispute that tore the Christian world asunder, the dispute between the Reformers and the Catholics. Though the Reformation may have had its roots in the complaints about Church abuses and practices, and about interpretations of various passages in Scripture and of various Church doctrines, after the Leipzig Disputation (1519) a central issue became that of determining how one gains religious knowledge, and of telling how one ascertains if it is true. Luther and his followers rejected some of the religious knowledge claims of the Church and also the criterion by which these claims were validated. At Leipzig Luther announced that he was unperturbed that some of his views were those held by heretics who had been condemned by Church Councils and the Pope. He then began to assert that religious knowledge claims are not authenticated by the authority of the Pope or Councils, but by conscience and the inner experience one feels on reading Scripture, and on being affected by the Holy Spirit.[6] For both Luther and Calvin the criterion of religious knowledge became one's subjective experience.

Various Catholic defenders then began to contend that once the Reformers had abandoned the accepted religious knowledge criterion of the Church they would be led into a complete scep-

---

[6]See Luther's opinions at Leipzig, in the *Babylonish Captivity of the Church* and at the Diet of Worms, as cited in *Documents of the Christian Church*, ed. Henry Bettenson (New York and London, 1947), pp. 271–85.

ticism, "a sink of uncertainty and error." They saw, as a result of reading the newly rediscovered text of Sextus Empiricus,[7] that the Reformers would immediately be forced into the Pyrrhonian problem of the criterion and would be unable to justify their criterion. Without this they would always remain uncertain and could not tell if anything could be known. The Reformers, in turn, saw that the same problems could be turned against the Catholics, in that the Catholics could not justify *their* criterion of authority and the oral and written traditions. The puzzles about authenticating a criterion would apply just as much to an old as to a new one, and the Catholics would find themselves as uncertain about religious knowledge as they claimed the Protestants were.

In the course of the running debate between the Catholics and Reformers, the problem grew to be a general sceptical one—could anything at all be known? Building on materials from the Greek sceptics, the Catholics developed a "new machine of war" to devastate the Protestants by showing step by step that nothing could be known by the standards of the Reformers, and that each individual Protestant would be reduced to affirming his own uncertain, subjective opinions, with no basis whatsoever for them. The Protestants saw that this sort of attack also could be turned against their opponents, as well as against anyone claiming to have any kind of knowledge based on sense or rational evidence. From Gentian Hervet, a French Counter-Reformation leader who published the first Latin edition of Sextus Empiricus' works, to Juan Maldonado, the first Jesuit to teach at the University of Paris (and a friend of Montaigne), to St. François de Sales, to Cardinal Du Perron, to the Jesuits Jean Gontery and François Veron (the latter a teacher at La Flèche in Descartes' day), the sceptical machine of war was developed and perfected.[8] The Catholics challenged whether the Protestants could determine what book is the Bible, or, if they could, what it says or what it means.

[7]The *Adversus Mathematicos* of Sextus Empiricus was translated into Latin and published in 1569 by the leading French Counter-Reformer, Gentian Hervet, as a way of answering the Calvinists.

[8]On the "machine of war," see R. H. Popkin, *The History of Scepticism from Erasmus to Descartes* (rev. ed.; Assen, The Netherlands, 1964), pp. 67–74; "Skepticism and the Counter-Reformation in France," *Archiv für Reformationsgeschichte*, LI (1960), 58–87.

They challenged what criteria could be employed, and whether these criteria could be proven to be reliable. They pointed out that the data gained by sense experience are questionable and that some criterion is needed to determine which sense experiences were veridical and which not. They pointed out that the employment of the human faculties of reasoning and judgment to tell what, if anything, the Bible said (some challenged whether one could really tell that the marks on the pages were words or not[9]), just raised further problems about criteria of right reasoning, criteria for correct application of the criteria, etc. And when the Catholics' machine of war finally drove the Reformers back to their own subjective inner experience as the ultimate court of appeal, the Catholics pointed out that the Reformers had no way of telling whether this experience was delusive or not. Any appeals to their own convictions would only be circular and unsatisfactory. So, if religious knowledge was to be found by examining Scripture and recognizing the truth by one's own inner experience, the Catholics claimed that the sceptical problems would prevent the Protestants from ever being certain either of what book contained the true message, or what that message was, or what should be done about it. For the Protestants, the Catholics contended, all would remain in doubt. And since the Protestants admitted that they were all fallible, they could never have any complete assurance.

The Protestants in turn pointed out that the same sceptical crisis could be developed for the Catholics. As they were strongly pressed by professional arguers like Father Veron, the Protestants cried out that if the sceptical attack were taken seriously it would undermine all confidence in everything and destroy all certitude that rested upon the senses or reason. And if the same kinds of sceptical arguments were applied with regard to the religious knowledge claims of the Catholics, based on documents, pronouncements, etc., and against the Catholic criteria, the Protestants claimed their opponents would also find themselves completely in doubt about what was true or false in religion.[10] The English theologian William Chillingworth originally found

[9] This point was raised by John Sergeant in his *Sure-Footing in Christianity* (London, 1665), p. 68.

[10] On the Protestant answers, see Popkin, *History of Scepticism*, pp. 75–79.

himself pushed from Anglicanism to Catholicism by the sceptical arguments. Then, by applying the same reasonings, he found Catholicism too dubious to adhere to. (The same sort of thing happened to the Calvinist Pierre Bayle, who by sceptical arguments reasoned his way in and out of Catholicism.) Chillingworth then marshaled the arguments of his favorite book, the writings of Sextus Empiricus, into a devastating sceptical attack on the Catholic claims to religious knowledge.[11] Perhaps the high point of this kind of polemic was the book *Of the Incurable Scepticism of the Church of Rome* by the late seventeenth-century Calvinist Jean La Placette. In this work La Placette argued that the Catholic Church could have at most one member who could be sure of his faith, namely, the Pope. Every other member must rely on what the Pope says. But how do they tell who is the Pope? They have only sensory reports and written documents to lead them to an answer. But these reports and documents can be false or misleading, or they can be perceived mistakenly by one's unreliable senses. And, since all Catholics except the Pope admit to being fallible, they can always err in their interpretations and evaluations of the material at their disposal. Hence, La Placette claimed, all Catholics, save the Pope, should be in doubt about their faith.[12]

One of the results of this sceptical challenge and counter-challenge was the emergence of a movement of Christian sceptics claiming that their religion was based solely on faith and not on any evidence or reasoning. The Christian sceptics claimed, whether sincerely or not, that their view, from Montaigne down to Bayle and Bishop Huet, was the same as that of St. Paul, who rejected Greek philosophic standards as the measure of religious truth and who insisted on the primacy of pure faith.[13] Religious knowl-

[11]See William Chillingworth, *The Religion of Protestants, A Safe Way to Salvation,* in *The Works of William Chillingworth* (London, 1704).

[12]Jean La Placette, *Of the Incurable Scepticism of the Church of Rome* (London, 1688); the Latin original is *De Insanabili romanae Ecclesiae Scepticismo, dissertatio qua demonstratur nihil omnino esse quod firma fide persuadere sibi pontificii possint* (Amsterdam, 1696). Two similar works are J. A. Turretin, *Pyrrhonismus Pontificus* (Leyden, 1692), and David-Renaud Boullier, *Le Pyrrhonisme de l'Eglise Romaine* (Amsterdam, 1757).

[13]See, for instance, François La Mothe Le Vayer's claim that St. Paul was preaching scepticism in his *Prose Chagrine,* in *Oeuvres* (Paris, 1669), IX, 359–60.

edge based only on faith, the Christian sceptics claimed, was impervious to the sceptical onslaught. Instead, sceptical arguments could be seen as the preparation for true faith, as they eliminated all false or dubious views and left the mind "blank, nude and ready" for God to write upon. The sceptic could not be a heretic, observed Montaigne's disciple, Father Pierre Charron, since, in holding no views except those that God had given him, he could not hold the wrong views.[14]

Christian scepticism or fideism flourished from the mid-sixteenth century until the end of the seventeenth century. It was usually a Catholic position, appearing in a wide range of writers from Montaigne and Maldonado to Pascal and Bishop Huet (and then in revived form in post-Revolutionary arch-conservative writers like De Maistre and Lamennais). Its most irrational statement was offered by the Protestant Pierre Bayle,[15] presenting the view in such an extreme way as to convince his eighteenth-century admirers that he was really a complete unbeliever. The view appears even in so un-Christian a writer as David Hume, who could say, probably ironically, that the first and most essential step toward becoming a true and believing Christian is to become a philosophical sceptic.[16]

If scepticism became a fundamental issue in the sixteenth century due to the controversies between the Reformers and the Catholics over the nature and reliability of contending claims about religious knowledge, the form in which scepticism was to affect the development of modern philosophy was the result, I believe, of the more generalized statements of the sceptical case offered by Montaigne, by his distant cousin Francisco Sanches, and by his disciple Pierre Charron. All three claimed to be Christian sceptics of Catholic persuasion (though Montaigne's mother was a Spanish Jewess, and Sanches was born in Portugal, the son

---

[14]See Pierre Charron, *La Sagesse,* in *Toutes les Oeuvres de Pierre Charron* (Paris, 1635), Book II, chap. ii, p. 22.

[15]See, for example, Bayle's statement of this view in articles "Paulicians," Remark E, "Pyrrho," Remarks B and C, and the "Third Clarification," in his *Historical and Critical Dictionary,* trans. Richard H. Popkin, with the assistance of Craig Brush (Indianapolis, 1965).

[16]David Hume, *Dialogues Concerning Natural Religion,* ed. Norman Kemp-Smith (London and Edinburgh, 1947), p. 228.

of a prominent Jewish family who had to flee to France to escape the torments of the Inquisition). Charron had started out as a sceptical Counter-Reformer, offering Pyrrhonian arguments against atheists, Jews, Mohammedans, and especially against Calvinists. All of them lived and wrote in a world in constant turmoil over religious controversies.[17]

Montaigne in the "Apology for Raimond Sebond," Sanches in *Quod nihil scitur,* and Charron in *On Wisdom,* all generalized and modernized the sceptical case and used the refurbished Pyrrhonian arguments against all forms of knowledge claims, be they of the Scholastics, the Platonists, the Renaissance humanists, the Hellenistic philosophers, the Reformers, or the new scientists. Montaigne with his rambling style, Sanches with his incisive dialectic, and Charron with his didactic rendition of Montaigne, all revitalized the materials from Sextus and from Cicero's accounts of academic scepticism to cast doubt on whether we could ascertain if anything could be known in any area whatsoever, theology, philosophy, science, or anything else. They employed the tropes of the Pyrrhonists to question the reliability of sense information; they posed the dream problem to question the reality of experience. They used the classical sceptical arguments to question whether adequate or sufficient evidence could ever be offered to substantiate any view. They forcefully posed the problem of ever finding any satisfactory criterion to employ for adjudicating either our sense information or our judgments about anything, and they pressed the sceptical ploy that one would either need an infinite series of criteria or would be forced into circular reasoning in the attempt to justify either man's senses or his reason as a source of reliable knowledge about the world. These three great sceptics of the late sixteenth century tried to show that in every area there were conflicting knowledge claims, and that given the human epistemological predicament there was no way of ascertaining what was *really* true. They developed a thoroughgoing scepticism with regard to the senses and the uses of reason by posing apparently unanswerable questions and difficulties concerning the evaluation of sense data and rational con-

[17]On Montaigne, Sanches, and Charron, see Popkin, *History of Scepticism,* pp. 38–63, and the articles on each of them by the same author in *The Encyclopedia of Philosophy,* ed. Paul Edwards (New York, 1967).

clusions and judgments. They tried to show that human knowledge claims are actually only dubious human opinions, and that the attempt to know reality is about as successful, as Montaigne claimed, as the attempt to clutch water.

For Montaigne, Sanches, and Charron, scepticism was not merely a tactical way of disarming and destroying the dogmatists who thought they knew something about the nature of the world around them. It was also the only attitude to adopt in the face of the human knowledge situation. The more one probed and laid bare what was involved in the attempt to know anything, the more dubious the whole cognitive enterprise became. One was left with what Pascal later called "the misery of man without God," uncertainty about everything, uncertainty about where our information comes from, what it is about, and whether or not it is reliable. Instead of trying to maintain some dogmatical theory about the world, they recommended adopting the Pyrrhonian suspense of judgment about anything beyond appearances as the most viable result of exploring the state of human knowledge. They all professed a Christian scepticism, a fideism, as the only *real* way out. Faith and revelation alone could provide any genuine assurance and any basis for understanding the world.

Montaigne and Charron and their followers regarded the developing scientific enterprises in astronomy, medicine, chemistry, physics, etc. as just one more dogmatic effort to accomplish the impossible, to know the nature of reality. They were not impressed by the scientific revolution going on around them, seeing it as just the replacement of one set of dubious opinions by another such set. They recommended abandoning scientific research along with other misguided efforts to find out what is really going on.[18] One of the last of the Montaignians, and Descartes' contemporary, François La Mothe Le Vayer, wrote a discourse on the use of scepticism for the sciences. Instead of contending that scepticism could help clarify scientific findings, or could help by eliminating false or dubious theories, La Mothe Le Vayer argued that scepticism could be of use by undermining any confidence at all in scientific research and by eliminating any interest or concern

[18]See, for instance, Montaigne's remarks on the new scientists in the "Apologie de Raimond Sebond," *Les Essais de Michel de Montaigne* (Villey edition; Paris, 1922), II, 325–27, which are repeated by Charron, and by Bishop Jean-Pierre Camus in his "Essay sceptique" of 1603.

with science.[19] The tradition stemming from Montaigne by and large saw scepticism primarily as a destructive force that would wash away all theories and theorizing, would undermine all human intellectual endeavors, and would leave mankind purged of epistemological poisons resulting from its dogmatic attempts to know.

In contrast to this anti-intellectual, destructive form of scepticism that flourished in the first half of the seventeenth century, another form developed from Sanches, that of constructive or mitigated scepticism. From his sceptical analysis of man's epistemological plight, Sanches suggested that from the conclusion *nihil sciri,* nothing can be known, that, *per non sequitur,* one should try to gain what information one can about the world from a patient, careful inspection of particulars and a cautious judgment or interpretation of them. In his view, a kind of rudimentary empirical scientific activity is what is left once we realize that we cannot gain knowledge about reality.[20] Sanches, who apparently coined the term "scientific method,"[21] saw empirical science as the potentially fruitful issue of the sceptical crisis. His constructive scepticism was developed by Gassendi as a *via media* between scepticism and dogmatism that could provide a "shadow of truth," a hypothetical picture of the world;[22] by Pascal in his scientific works and his examination of the geometrical method as a way of gaining the best possible theories to interpret the empirical world,[23] and by the early Royal Society

[19]François La Mothe Le Vayer, "Discours pour montrer que les doutes de la philosophie sceptique sont de grand usage dans les sciences," in *Oeuvres,* XV, 65–124.

[20]See Francisco Sanches, *Quod nihil scitur* in *Opera philosophica,* ed. Joaquim de Carvalho (Coimbra, 1955), pp. 47–53.

[21]There is a lost work of Sanches' with the title *De Método Universal de las Ciencias,* apparently written in 1578. This may be the first use of the term "scientific method." On the history of "method" in modern philosophy, see Neil W. Gilbert, *Renaissance Concepts of Method* (New York, 1960), and the review of this work by Popkin in *Philosophy and Phenomenological Research,* XXIII (1962).

[22]See Pierre Gassendi, *Syntagma philosophicum, Logica,* esp. Liber II, cap. V, in *Opera* (Lyon, 1658). See also Popkin's article on Gassendi in the *Encyclopedia of Philosophy* and Bernard Rochot's "Gassendi et le Syntagma Philosophicum," *Revue de Synthèse,* LXVII (1950), 67–79.

[23]See Blaise Pascal's "Esprit geometrique," his letters to Père Noel on the vacuum, and the "Preface sur le traité du vide."

theoreticians as a justification for their "experimental philosophy."[24]

Renaissance scepticism, whether constructive or destructive, unleashed a sceptical crisis throughout the European intellectual world. The extension of the scepticism employed in the religious controversies to all areas of human knowledge undermined confidence and assurance in the knowledge claims that had been and were being made. Montaigne, who was so sensitive to the many forces that were eroding man's certainty during the sixteenth century, could portray so vividly the plight of the late Renaissance intellectual in "painting himself." Montaigne could make his personal sceptical crisis the picture of modern man, in doubt about everything, unable to find any certainty except through faith and revelation (and there is some reason to doubt that Montaigne himself found any help by these means). The doubts posed by Montaigne, by Sanches, and by Charron apparently overwhelmed their contemporaries. The rapidly changing world of the sixteenth century came to its conclusion with the whole intellectual fabric having been unraveled, and with sceptical questions posing seemingly insurmountable difficulties in the quest for knowledge and certainty.

In the early seventeenth century, a sceptical atmosphere seems to have been all pervasive, at least in France and England. The works of Montaigne and Charron were constantly being reissued and were being read by avant-garde intellectuals.[25] The sceptical classics of Sextus and Cicero were being studied assiduously.[26] In Paris, then the hub of the intellectual world, the Montaignians were at the very center of the court and of society. Montaigne's

---

[24]Cf. the theory of scientific knowledge advanced by Joseph Glanvill in his *Essays on Several Important Subjects in Philosophy and Religion* (London, 1676) and by John Wilkins in his *Of the Principles and Duties of Natural Religion* (London, 1675). These two works will soon appear in photoreproduction editions in the series *Texts in Early Modern Philosophy,* ed. R. H. Popkin, published by the Johnson Reprint Corporation. On the Royal Society theory of limited scepticism, see Henry Van Leeuwen, *The Problem of Certainty in English Thought, 1630–1690* (The Hague, 1963).

[25]See Alan M. Boase, *The Fortunes of Montaigne, A History of the Essays in France, 1580–1699* (London, 1935).

[26]The writings of both these authors are cited by many of the thinkers of the time. The editions of Sextus' works are discussed in Popkin, *History of Scepticism,* pp. 17–19.

adopted daughter, Mlle. de Gournay, ran one of the great salons,[27] and various sceptics held high office in the Church and state.[28] When a Jesuit, François Garasse, tried to bring about a suppression of the Pyrrhonism of Montaigne and Charron on the basis of the irreligion he claimed it had inspired, he found that most powerful and orthodox Church interests were willing and eager to protect the sceptics and to insist that their message was the true Christianity of St. Paul and St. Augustine.[29] In the 1620s writers began to appear to try to challenge the "nouveaux Pyrrhoniens," and from their picture one would gather that scepticism was a most lively force, then very much *au courant* on the intellectual scene.[30]

In the period 1620–30, perhaps the most avant-garde French philosopher was Pierre Gassendi, a prodigy who began lecturing by the time he was sixteen years old. He was a priest, a scientist of some renown, a coworker with Galileo, and by the 1620s a philosophy professor. He was strongly influenced by Sextus, Montaigne, Sanches, and Charron.[31] His first work, published in 1624, was a set of arguments, based on his sceptical readings, against Aristotelian philosophy, which he presumably taught at Aix-en-Provence. The second book of this work, not published until much later though written at this time, developed a complete sceptical attack not only against Aristotelianism, but against all forms of dogmatic philosophy. In the last chapter, entitled "That there is

[27]On Mlle. de Gournay, see Mario Schiff, *La Fille d'alliance de Montaigne, Marie de Gournay* (Paris, 1910).

[28]Gabriel Naudé was librarian to Richelieu and Mazarin and secretary to Cardinal Bagni; Guy Patin was the rector of the medical school of the Sorbonne; Leonard Marandé was one of Richelieu's secretaries; François La Mothe Le Vayer was the teacher of the king's brother and a royal counselor; Pierre Gassendi became the professor of mathematics at the Collège Royal.

[29]Father Garasse's campaign against scepticism was successfully opposed by the Jansenist leader Jean Duvergier du Hauranne (Saint-Cyran). On this episode, see Popkin, *History of Scepticism*, pp. 114–18.

[30]These early attacks on scepticism are discussed in chapters 6 and 8 of Popkin's *History of Scepticism*.

[31]On Gassendi's career, see Bernard Rochot's article "La Vie, le caractère et la formation intellectuelle" in the Centre International de Synthèse volume, *Pierre Gassendi, 1592–1655, sa vie et son oeuvre* (Paris, 1955); and René Pintard, *Le Libertinage érudit dans la première moitié du XVIIe siècle* (Paris, 1943), pp. 147–56.

no science, and especially no Aristotelian science," Gassendi employed the arguments from Sextus to show that human knowledge is always restricted to how things appear, and can never reach their real natures, the things-in-themselves. Gassendi offered the distinction between primary qualities, the real features of a thing, and secondary qualities, how the thing appears to us, and he insisted we could know only the latter. Therefore, he contended, we could never have any science, that is, necessary knowledge about the real world. From appearances, we have no basis for judging or inferring what real objects may be like. The sceptical problems about sense experience make it impossible for us to describe or define a real object on the basis of our perceptions. The sceptical problems about reasoning prevent us from being able to infer from what we experience to what reality may be like. And since we cannot even establish a satisfactory criterion of true knowledge, we cannot ascertain what a genuine science would be like. All that one can conclude, according to Gassendi, is that *nihil sciri,* nothing can be known.[32]

Though Gassendi became more moderate in his scepticism, and in later works offered what he called a *via media* between scepticism and dogmatism, and proposed his Epicureanism as a hypothesis for relating different aspects of the world of sense experience, he nevertheless was a leading sceptical force in the period 1620–30, attacking all sorts of dogmatisms, old and new. He was also a close friend of the sceptics living in Paris, and a member of their group, the *Tétrade.*[33] He was one of the most powerful intellectuals of this period.

Another who contributed greatly to the sceptical atmosphere of the time was Descartes' and Gassendi's close friend, Father Marin Mersenne. After studying at La Flèche a few years before Descartes, Mersenne joined the pious order of the Minimes in Paris. In the mid-1620s he published a series of enormous tracts against the enemies of science and religion, the atheists (he

[32]See Pierre Gassendi, *Dissertations en forme de paradoxes contre les Aristoteliciens (Exercitationes Paradoxicae adversus Aristoteleos),* ed. and trans. Bernard Rochot (Paris, 1959), esp. Book II, Diss. 6. (Part of this appears in English translation in *The Philosophy of the Sixteenth and Seventeenth Centuries,* ed. R. H. Popkin [New York, 1966]).

[33]This informal society is discussed at length in Pintard's *Libertinage érudit,* esp. Tome I, 2ᵉ partie, chap. 1, and 3ᵉ partie.

claimed Paris alone had 60,000, which was then the estimated population of the city), the deists, the alchemists, the Renaissance naturalists, the cabalists, *and* the Pyrrhonians. After such an ambitious beginning, Mersenne devoted the rest of his life to the more constructive task of being the chief propagandist for the new science, and of being a one-man society for the advancement of science, by publishing textbooks, translations of Galileo, and scientific compendia, by encouraging many of the leading lights on the scene, like Gassendi, Descartes, and Hobbes, and by carrying on a vast correspondence keeping everyone informed of the latest scientific developments. Mersenne probably contributed more than anyone else of the time to increasing the knowledge of and interest in current scientific developments.[34]

In *La Verité des sciences contre les septiques ou pyrrhoniens* (1625), a tract on scepticism of over 1,000 pages, Mersenne presented a dialogue between an alchemist, a sceptic, and a Christian philosopher (presumably himself). The sceptic uses the weapons of Sextus Empiricus as a means of destroying the alchemist's claims to knowledge. The first book includes a summary of most of Sextus' *Outlines of Pyrrhonism,* along with Mersenne's commentary on the arguments. His usual response is not to answer the sceptic's challenge, but rather to say "So what?" For Mersenne, the doubts raised by the Pyrrhonists may not be capable of resolution, our knowledge may not be justifiable, but that in no way leads us to doubt of the knowledge itself. Our sense experiences may vary, but that does not impugn any of the experiences, nor does it prevent us from finding lawful relations that connect our varying experiences; for example, the law of refraction provides us with a relationship between our experience of seeing an oar bent in water, and one straight when removed from the water. We may not know which is the *real* oar, but we still know something and can make predictions based on this knowledge. Similarly, the dream problem doesn't prevent us from knowing what the world looks like when we are in what we call a waking state. The sceptic keeps pressing the point that nothing in Mersenne's response shows that we actually know the real natures of things, their essences. But Mersenne keeps pointing out that that is not necessary in order for us to know something,

[34]On Mersenne's life and career, see Robert Lenoble, *Mersenne ou la naissance du mécanisme* (Paris, 1943), pp. 15–59.

and to know something that can provide an adequate guide for us in this vale of tears. Sceptical doubts notwithstanding, Mersenne contended, we still do know a great deal about the world of experience.[35] The last three-fourths of the dialogue is a recital of what, in fact, is known in mathematics and science. The sceptic gives in under this avalanche of knowledge. But Mersenne kept indicating, especially in his later works, that he himself was a complete epistemological sceptic with regard to our ability to know anything about reality. In answer to the question "Can one know anything certain in physics or mathematics?" Mersenne insisted the answer was "No." We can only know about appearances and about hypothetical relationships, never about essences or things-in-themselves.[36]

Thus Mersenne offered a new way of dealing with the rising force of scepticism, namely, by accepting its arguments as decisive about the possibility of metaphysical knowledge, while showing that in a positivistic and pragmatic sense the sceptical arguments in no way prevented us from having useful knowledge about the world of appearance or experience, knowledge which did not become dubious just because we could not know the world beyond experience.

In the period just before Descartes' appearance on the scene, Gassendi and Mersenne were among the most influential thinkers of the time. Their scepticism or partial scepticism was infused into the world of the "new scientists" and the avant-garde theologians, into the world of those who had broken with Scholasticism. Descartes' first known public philosophical discussion occurred at a gathering of sceptics in the home of the Papal Nuncio in Paris in 1628 at which Mersenne was present. An alchemist, Chandoux, was giving a talk about the low state of learning in the schools. From the two accounts we have of this meeting, Chandoux's speech was a typical sceptical dirge. Everyone present, including two cardinals, applauded his views, except

---

[35]Marin Mersenne, *La Verité des sciences contre les septiques ou pyrrhoniens* (Paris, 1625), Book I.

[36]Mersenne, *Questions inouyes ou récréation des scavans* (Paris, 1634), pp. 69–71; and *Les Questions théologiques, physiques, morales et mathématiques* (Paris, 1634). On Mersenne's form of scepticism, see R. H. Popkin, "Father Mersenne's War Against Pyrrhonism," *Modern Schoolman*, XXXIV (1956–57), 61–68; and his *History of Scepticism,* pp. 132–43.

for René Descartes. When Descartes was asked for his opinions, he replied by criticizing the fact that the speaker and the audience were willing to settle for less than complete certainty, and that they were willing to accept probabilities that might possibly be false. Descartes claimed he had a method that would avoid these difficulties. Cardinal Bérulle, who was at the meeting, then encouraged Descartes to work out his method.[37] Descartes returned to Holland where, according to the autobiographical account in the *Discourse on Method,* he applied the method of doubt to his beliefs and opinions and found the truth that was so unshakeable that no argument of the sceptics could make him doubt it.[38] From that point he was able to go on and build his new metaphysical system.

In terms of this background, I submit that Descartes saw most clearly that the sceptics of the Renaissance and of his time had raised a special kind of challenge. They had questioned all of man's knowledge claims, all of the means of gaining knowledge, and all of the means for ascertaining the reliability and certainty of human knowledge. By introducing the demon problem, Descartes was able to push the matter still further. Once this problem was taken seriously, Descartes could show that if such an evil force existed, even the surest, the most evident truths could be doubted, since the demon might be deceiving us, no matter how certain we felt.

In the light of this super-scepticism, Descartes saw that the sceptical crisis could not be resolved by applying means from within a challenged and questioned system to the issues raised. Hence the attempts of some of his contemporaries to use Aristotle's theory of knowledge to answer scepticism could not be satisfactory. He also saw that those like Herbert of Cherbury and Francis Bacon, who were going to solve the sceptical problems by the use of new techniques and instruments, would not really come to grips with what was at issue.[39] He was aware that

[37]This meeting is discussed in Adrien Baillet, *Vie de M. Descartes* (Table Ronde edition; Paris, 1946), pp. 70–74, and in Descartes' letter to Villebressieu, 1631, in René Descartes, *Oeuvres,* ed. Charles Adam and Paul Tannery (Paris, 1897), I, 213.

[38]Descartes, *Discours,* in *Oeuvres,* VI, 30–32.

[39]On Herbert of Cherbury's answer to scepticism, see Popkin, *History of Scepticism,* chap. 8.

instead the issues had to be resolved in their own terms, by show-ing that the sceptical problems could be overcome through scep-ticism itself.

He thus applied his sceptical method of doubt, and claimed that this sceptical research revealed that there is true knowledge—the *cogito*—that cannot possibly be doubted; that this true knowledge revealed the criterion of knowledge, that whatever is clearly and distinctly perceived is true; that this criterion can be guaranteed by God, who is definitely not a deceiver; and that through the employment of this criterion it is possible to ascertain the limits and the reliability of various knowledge claims, whether they be empirical or rational.

The structure of the Cartesian answer to scepticism, and the problems raised in the construction of this answer, have created that complex of issues I have labeled the modern problem of knowledge, such as the problem of whether we can know that an external world exists, or whether we can know that there are other minds, or whether we can know anything with certainty beyond immediate experience or logical tautologies, etc. Descartes' answer was obviously designed to justify the claim that what he took to be the new kind of knowledge then being discovered, the mechanistic physics of Galileo and Descartes, was both true and certain. Nonetheless, his answer is structured to respond to the sceptical challenge, and he claimed in his reply to Father Bourdin that he, Descartes, was the first to overthrow the doubts of the sceptics.[40] It is an answer that is formulated in terms of the scep-tical problems, and the weaknesses in his answer can be seen in terms of his failure to *really* resolve the questions the sceptics had raised. Some of his immediate critics, like Bourdin, Schook, and Voetius, showed that he had actually become so sceptical in his method that he really could not overcome doubt, even by the *cogito*.[41] Others of a more sceptical bent, like Gassendi and Mer-senne, and later Bayle and Bishop Huet, argued that his whole

---

[40]Descartes, *Objectiones Septimae cum Notis Authoris sive Dissertatio de Prima Philosophia,* in *Oeuvres,* VII, 550.

[41]See Bourdin's remarks in the *Seventh Objections,* esp. *Oeuvres,* VII, 528–29. (In Descartes, *Philosophical Works,* ed. Elizabeth S. Haldane and G. R. T. Ross [New York, 1955], this appears in II, 318–19.) Martin Schoock and Gisbert Voetius of Utrecht attacked Descartes in *Admiranda methodus novae philosophiae Renati Des Cartes* (Utrecht, 1643).

system after the *cogito* would collapse under sceptical probing, and that he finally could not be sure of any truths or of any world, and that in fact, Descartes, the self-announced conquerer of scepticism, was just unfortunately a *sceptique malgré lui*.[42] And the problems these sceptical critics saw as unresolved are those that have constituted the core of the modern problem of knowledge ever since.

The epistemological battles from the time of Descartes down to the days of Hume and Kant have been, I would contend, not just, or even centrally, a series of attempts to improve upon Descartes' theory by such philosophical geniuses as Hobbes, Spinoza, Leibniz, Malebranche, Locke, Berkeley, Hume, and Kant. Rather they have been a series of responses to the many new forms the sceptical challenge was taking during this period as the living sceptics, from Gassendi to Foucher, to Bayle, to Huet, to Hume, attacked each attempt to construct an epistemology that would answer the special and far-reaching sceptical onslaught upon the knowledge claims of the "new philosophers."[43] Scepticism is the specter that has been haunting Western philosophy since Descartes' time. The various great systems each try in their own way to find some means of burying this ghost and achieving some kind of certainty that can *really* be relied upon.

To sum up, the great developments during the Renaissance and the Reformation spawned a fundamental kind of rejection of all

[42] See Pierre Gassendi, *Disquisitio Metaphysica, seu Dubitationes et Instantiae adversus Renati Cartesii Metaphysicam et Reponsa,* ed. with French translation by Bernard Rochot (Paris, 1959) ; Pierre-Daniel Huet, *Censura Philosophiae Cartesianae* (Paris, 1689) ; and Bayle's many attacks on Cartesianism in the *Historical and Critical Dictionary,* esp. article "Pyrrho," Remark B. Mersenne's objections appear in the *Secondes Objections,* in Descartes' *Oeuvres,* IX, esp. 99–100.

[43] On this later portion of the history of scepticism, see R. H. Popkin, "The High Road to Pyrrhonism," *American Philosophical Quarterly,* II (1965) 1–15; "Leibniz and the French Sceptics," *Revue Internationale de Philosophie,* Numéro 76–77 (1966), pp. 228–48; "The Sceptical Crisis and the Rise of Modern Philosophy, III," *Review of Metaphysics,* VII (1953–54), 499–510; "Scepticism in the Enlightenment," *Transactions of the 1st International Congress on the Enlightenment* (Geneva, 1963), pp. 1321–45; and article "Scepticism" in the *Encyclopedia of Philosophy.* See also Van Leeuwen, *The Problem of Certainty in English Thought,* and Richard A. Watson, *The Downfall of Cartesianism, 1673–1712* (The Hague, 1966).

previous and then contemporary ways of gaining knowledge, and of providing justifications of that knowledge. The implications of such a rejection, which I call the sceptical crisis, were made clear and vital to the intellectual world by Montaigne, Sanches, Charron, and Gassendi. By the 1620s they had thoroughly infected the philosophical world with their doubts. The sceptical problems they had posed then gave rise to modern epistemology in the work of Descartes. After this, the continuous attacks of the sceptics in the seventeenth and eighteenth centuries on the theories of Descartes and those of his successors shaped the problems of modern epistemology, and also shaped the kinds of answers it was able to provide to the sceptical problems. I think that one can trace the march from Descartes to Kant in terms of this ceaseless battle between the sceptics and the new philosophers, each new theory purporting to resolve the sceptical difficulties that the preceding one failed to resolve, and each new theory then being assaulted with a new sceptical barrage.

In the broadest terms I would claim that the sceptical crisis of the Renaissance and Reformation, and its effects on modern thought from Descartes down to Husserl and Wittgenstein and Sartre, has reverberated throughout the struggles of modern epistemology. Can anything *really* be known? Can we *really* be certain of anything? Or are we, as Pascal said, lost in "a sink of uncertainty and error"? The possibility that the human situation could actually be this dreadful was posed by the sceptics of the sixteenth and seventeenth centuries. The attempt to overcome this haunting sceptical vision and to replace it with a more serene one, has, for better or for worse, been one of the dynamic forces in the history of epistemology from Descartes onward. Seeing the development of epistemology in terms of this struggle with scepticism provides some insight into our present situation, and may make us more aware of where we are and where we have been.

Thinking and Doing

ROBERT J. FOGELIN

I

In a brief, and distressingly incomplete, account of the practical syllogism, Aristotle traces out a connection between thought and action. He tells us that what happens seems parallel to the case of thinking and inferring about the immovable objects of science:

> There the end is the truth seen (for, when one conceives the two premisses, one at once conceives and comprehends the conclusion), but here the two premisses result in a conclusion which is an action—for example, one conceives that every man ought to walk, one is a man oneself: straightway one walks; . . .

A bit later he says this:

> . . . the actualizing of desire is a substitute for inquiry or reflection. I want to drink, says appetite; this is a drink, says sense or imagination or mind: straightway I drink. In this way living creatures are impelled to move and to act, and desire is the last or immediate cause of movement, and desire arises after perception or after imagination and conception.[1]

Examined closely, these passages admit of two very different interpretations. The first I shall call the obvious interpretation; the second, the interesting interpretation. I shall not try to decide which interpretation best fits the text as a whole; I shall only ferret out the interesting interpretation and then—setting Aristotle's text aside—explore it in its own right.

The obvious interpretation goes something like this: Aristotle

[1]Aristotle, *De Motu Animalium,* trans. A. S. Farquharson, in *The Works of Aristotle* (London, 1912), Vol. V, chap. 7.

pairs off various components of a theoretical syllogism with various psychological components. He then suggests that the action itself follows from these psychological components in much the same way that a conclusion follows from a set of premises. The parallel looks like this:

(A)   All M is P.   I want a drink.

         All S is M.   This is drink.

∴   All S is P.   ∴   Glug, glug, glug.

Somewhat dogmatically, I shall say that Aristotle's text is only minimally illuminating under the obvious interpretation. It does suggest that human actions are connected with thought and desire in a way that is not simply contingent. It does not, however, reveal anything about the structure of this noncontingent connection.

The interesting interpretation takes its cue from Aristotle's initial phrasing. There the analogue is not an argument, but instead a *process* of reasoning. We might spell out this process of thinking and inferring about the immovable objects of science in the following way:

(B) (1)   Comprehending that all M is P, and that all S is M, Mr. So & So reflected as follows:

     (2)   All M is P.

            All S is M.

     ∴   All S is P.

         and (3) straightway comprehended that all S is P. We now unfold the analogy by pairing off the act of drinking, not with the conclusion of the embedded argument, but instead with the "mental act" of comprehending the truth of this conclusion via argument.

The interesting interpretation is on a par with the obvious interpretation in being at least minimally illuminating: it too suggests that the connection between thought and action is somehow more than contingent. Beyond this, the interesting interpretation presents a more natural analogy: the mental act of comprehending is on a par with the physical act of drinking in a way that the proposition "All S is P" is not on a par with any physical act. Finally, the interesting interpretation is interesting, for it traces out a very rich system of connections. Without worrying about Aristotle's true intentions, I propose to exploit the interesting interpretation for all it is worth. The result, I think, will be an outline for a theory of human action.

II

Our task is to construct a pattern for thought passing into action that mirrors the schema for thinking and inferring about the immovable objects of science. Part of this pattern can be filled in with little difficulty:

(C) (1) Comprehending that ⌀ is drink and . . . . ,
Mr. So & So reflected as follows:

(2) . . . .
⌀ is drink.

∴ . . . .

and (3) straightway he drank ⌀.

We must now find a plausible way of filling the blanks.

Once again, Aristotle helps us along. He says this about the premises of action: ". . . the premisses of action are of two kinds, of the good and of the possible."[2]

It is clear from his examples that by possibility Aristotle is thinking of the availability of an object of desire. ("This is drink," says sense or imagination or mind.) This in turn suggests that the major premise of the embedded argument is hypothetical with the minor premise satisfying its antecedent. The pattern now looks like this:

(D) (1) Comprehending that ⌀ is drink and if ⌀ is drink,
then . . . . , Mr. So & So reflected as
follows:

(2) If ⌀ is drink, ...
⌀ is drink.

∴ . . . .

(3) and straightway he drank ⌀.

How can we fill in the remaining blanks in a plausible way? Aristotle tells us that the major premise of action is about the good (in some examples he uses an ought statement), and this, following current fashion, suggests that the premise has a prescriptive force. A sweeping way of tying the whole pattern together is to fill the blanks with a suitable imperative, thus generating the following completed schema:

(E) (1) Comprehending that ⌀ is drink and accepting the
prescription, if ⌀ is drink, then drink it, Mr. So
& So reflects as follows:

[2]*Ibid.*

(2)   If ϕ is drink, then drink ϕ.
         ϕ is drink.
∴   Drink ϕ !
(3)   and straightway he drank ϕ.

Here the embedded argument exhibits a valid prescriptive inference but, even more importantly, the third component now
describes just that action which directly satisfies the prescriptive
conclusion of the embedded argument. Thus we have a systematic
connection between the commitments expressed in the first component and the actual event described in the third component via
inferences contained in the middle component.

It will prove convenient to have a name for this pattern: I shall
call it the Prescriptive Model for Human Action, since the use of
prescriptive components is its distinctive feature. Before exploit-
ing this model it is necessary to say some general things about
the nature of prescriptions.

III

As far as I can tell, philosophers have employed the notion of
a prescription in two different ways: as the generic name for a
class of speech acts, and as an abstract entity more or less on a
par with propositions. In the former case, commands, requests,
suggestions, etc. are thought of as different kinds of prescriptions
and the task, then, is to sort them out. This is a useful activity
since there is a temptation to take one of these species of prescriptive discourses as paradigmatic for all the rest.[3] The idea
of a prescription as an abstract entity is usually one of tacit
assumption rather than explicit avowal. We notice, for example,
that the very same thing can be prescribed in different speech
acts. A general may order a man to go, a friend suggest it, and
his wife request it; and for all the differences in these speech acts
they have this much in common: they express the same prescription, that the man go. It thus becomes natural when studying
prescriptive inferences to set aside all the pragmatic features
pertaining to speech acts that formulate prescriptions and instead
to concentrate upon the prescriptive content itself. In this way,

---

[3]For example, it would be hard to estimate the amount of harm done by
the assumption that moral (and legal) prescriptions have the character of
commands.

prescriptions take on the role for practical discourse that has traditionally been assigned to propositions in the examination of theoretical discourse.

In this essay I shall use the notion of prescription in an abstract-entity fashion. When the occasion arises to speak about prescriptive speech acts, we can simply use the device of calling them prescriptive speech acts (i.e., speech acts that express prescriptions). I have no clear idea about the correct analysis of the relationship between prescriptive speech acts and the prescriptions they express; I have the same trouble here as I have trying to understand the relationship between an assertive speech act and the assertion it expresses.[4] Here I want to endow prescriptions with all the rights and privileges traditionally assigned to propositions. In particular, I want to speak about prescriptions in isolation from the speech acts that might express them.

Some further ideas about prescriptions are more important for our present inquiry. In the course of developing the prescriptive model, I have spoken of Mr. So & So *accepting* a given prescription. In the model we find two kinds of prescriptions: the hypothetical prescription "If ϕ is drink, then drink ϕ," and the categorical prescription "Drink ϕ!" I shall adopt the following principle governing the acceptance of a categorical prescription: a person who accepts a categorical prescription will straightway act in accordance with that prescription unless something interferes with the execution of his act.[5] Thus, when Mr. So & So accepts the categorical prescription "Drink ϕ," he straightway drinks ϕ unless something interferes with his act. If something does interfere with his drinking ϕ, we will then say that he *tried* to drink ϕ.

It is important here to recognize the difference between *accepting* a categorical prescription and believing that a categorical prescription is *acceptable*. It is entirely possible for a person to

---

[4]Problems about abstract entities are not avoided by the simple refusal to use the traditional terminology that suggests them. For example, talking about statements instead of propositions carries some advantage; it underscores the fact that what is expressed by a sentence is a function of the context in which it is used. But still, the statement made and the act of stating are very different things. A statement is something made *in* the act of stating; thus, statements are not really very different from the older notion of a proposition.

[5]This will be modified in the concluding section of this essay.

believe that a prescription is justified, warranted, or what have you, and for all that not accept it. In different words, I want to insist upon the contrast between believing that one ought to do something and being committed to doing it. This difference can be brought out by contrasting the moral psychologies of Kant and Hare. For Hare, if there are no interfering factors, the mere fact that a person does not do something shows that on that occasion he did not believe he ought to do it. Kant's view is very different. We can imagine a world where people, by their nature, act in accordance with moral laws. For these beings, moral laws would have the status of *laws of nature,* and, in a manner of speaking, an ought would not emerge at all. For Kant, an ought emerges in our world precisely because we can acknowledge the legitimacy of a demand *without* thereby being conditioned to act in conformity with it. It is just this doctrine, I take it, that Hare wishes to deny, and here at least I am on the side of Kant rather than Hare.

In the model for human action we also speak about accepting a hypothetical prescription "If ⌀ is drink, then drink ⌀." A person could, of course, accept such a prescription but never drink. He is committed to drinking only those things that he *believes* to be drink, and it is conceivable that this condition may never be satisfied. The emphasis upon the word "believes" marks an obvious, but still important, point. It is tempting to say that a thirsty person will drink water if it is presented to him, but this is not correct. A thirsty person will not normally drink the presented water if he thinks it is baby oil or brine, and, conversely, he may drink baby oil or brine if he thinks, quite mistakenly, that it is water. It is not what the thing is, but what it is *taken to be* that counts in the determination of action with respect to it.

IV

Subject to all kinds of hedging, cheating, and taking back, I shall say that a statement formulates an act description if, and only if, the statement plays the role of the third component in the prescriptive model of human action. Of course, I do not mean that the statement must be prefaced by a recital of the items in the first two components, nor even that the person who makes the statement must have these two components before his mind. The prescriptive model is, after all, only a model, and its virtue is exhibited not by showing how things really are, but through mirroring and making intelligible fundamental features of act descriptions.

One point that emerges immediately is that act descriptions can not be identified merely by a reference to features of the sentences that are used to express them. In particular, I do not think that we will get very far by trying to collect a group of verbs that we might call action verbs. As a matter of fact we describe the performances of the lucid agent and the madman using pretty much the same verbs, and over a wide range we use many of these verbs to describe events that occur in the course of nature. It is not the verb, nor even the sentence as a whole, that counts; it is the use of the sentence in an appropriate setting that makes the difference.

Granting all this, it is still true that there are sentences that are normally used to formulate act descriptions and other sentences that are not normally used in this way. In most contexts the sentence "John dropped the franchise" would be taken as an act description, simply because dropping a franchise is a fairly sophisticated legal performance. In contrast, the statement "John dropped his pen" is not usually taken as an act description. Unless we think that there is something special afoot, it doesn't cross our minds to inquire into his *reasons* for dropping the pen. "He didn't have any reasons; the pen just slipped from his hand when he was jostled."[6] On occasion, however, we wish to reverse (or at least modify) such presumptions. We can do this in a variety of ways, but for the most part we do not accomplish this through changing the verb. Our language does not have a full stock of special verbs ready at hand to deal with every special occasion. Instead, this is normally accomplished through the device of adverbial modification. The sentence "John dropped his pen" is converted into an explicit act description simply by saying "John *intentionally* dropped his pen." Conversely, the presumed act description "John dropped the franchise" is significantly modified when converted to "John dropped the franchise through a mistake." In the former case we can inquire into reasons where

---

[6] Part of Freud's genius was to search for reasons (and find them) where others would never think to look. Freud, however, did not abandon the distinction between those things that people do and those things that happen to them; instead, he redrew the boundary for important theoretical reasons.

previously this seemed out of place; in the latter case a whole range of questions about reasons is declared off limits.

The situation is interestingly complicated, however. A human performance can fail to be a human act in various ways and to various degrees, and we have adverbs to mark these specific aberrations. On the other side, we have a stock of adverbs that we use to *counter* a presumption that a performance is not an act (or not fully an act). It was Austin's brilliant idea that an examination of such adverbs could cast light on the structure of human action. If I may use two barbarisms in one sentence, through the study of methods of actification and deactification our attention is drawn to the various components of a human act. Austin's procedure was, however, piecemeal—showing, perhaps, a warranted distrust of architectonic. Here I am proceeding in the reverse fashion: if the prescriptive model has any bearing upon the nature of human action, it should provide a framework for sorting out and clarifying the system of adverbs that are used to qualify human actions. Next I shall try to show that it can perform this job.

V

As I now see it, the adverb "intentionally" is simply the most general term for giving something the status of an act description, and the adverb "unintentionally" is the most general term for doing the opposite. Saying that something was done intentionally excludes, in one sweep, a whole range of potential qualifications; if something is done intentionally, then it is not done unknowingly, unwittingly, accidentally, mistakenly, inadvertently, and so on. Using Jonathan Bennet's terminology, the word "intentionally" is an "ellipsis excluder."[7] Extending Bennett's terminology, I shall call the word "unintentionally" an "ellipsis dummy." When I say that something was done unintentionally I indicate, without giving any special details, that the performance in some way falls short of act-hood.[8]

---

[7]Jonathan Bennett, " 'Real,' " in *Mind,* LXXV (1966), 504–507.

[8]It should also be clear, on this account, why it is not always appropriate to say of an act that it is either intentional or unintentional. Still following Jonathan Bennett, using an ellipsis excluder has a *point* only when there is some presumption to be countered. Saying of an ordinary intentional action that it is intentional can sound strange and even be misleading.

Ranging under the ellipsis excluder "intentionally" and under the ellipsis dummy "unintentionally" there is a whole family of terms that give more detailed information concerning the presented performance.

Intentionally	*Unintentionally*
knowingly	unknowingly
voluntarily	involuntarily
willingly	unwillingly
purposely	inadvertently
deliberately	accidentally
	mistakenly

The relationships between these terms are complicated: they do not always pair off neatly into contrasting couples, nor do the members of each group fit into an orderly genus species structure. About all that the members of the first group have in common is that they seem vaguely affirmative; members of the second group seem somehow vaguely negative. Due to the limits of space, I cannot consider all these terms, but a few illustrations will exhibit the general strategy.

What is involved in saying that Mr. So & So *knowingly* shot the Prime Minister? At the very least, this remark entails that at the time he knew it was the Prime Minister whom he was shooting. But does the entailment hold in the reverse direction; in other words, is the claim that someone did something knowingly *equivalent* to the claim that he knew (at the time) that he was doing it? It seems to me that the answer to this question is no, and a clue to the difference lies in the inarticulate notion that adverbs modify, qualify, or otherwise clarify the status of act descriptions they govern. Perhaps an example will bring this out. When Mr. So & So shot the Prime Minister, he might have known (by the way) that it was a man, wearing clothes, standing on the sidewalk before him, that he shot. Yet it seems completely wrong to say that he knowingly shot a man, wearing clothes, standing on the sidewalk before him, even though he knew all these things *about* the man he shot. None of these items of knowledge helps to clarify the character of the act in question, and for this reason, I suggest, they seem out of place as part of an adverbial construction.

My own suggestion is this: to say that someone knowingly ∅ed is to indicate that an item of knowledge entered into his practical reflection *in one way or another*. Suppose Mr. So & So shoots the Prime Minister because he believes that he is his wife's secret lover. The embedded practical reasoning might have the following form:

(F) If x is my wife's secret lover, shoot x!
      The Prime Minister is my wife's secret lover.
      This man is the Prime Minister.
∴   Shoot this man!

And straightway he (knowingly) shot the Prime Minister. Notice that in this example, the fact that the person was the Prime Minister was not relevant to Mr. So & So's *motives* in the shooting. We might try to bring this out by saying that he did not shoot the man *because* he was the Prime Minister, but, perhaps, *in spite of* this fact. In sum, then, the claim that someone knowingly ∅ed indicates that an item of knowledge entered (in some manner) into his practical reflections. The exact location of the item of knowledge in the practical reflection is not given by such a remark, but it is usually apparent in a concrete setting.

Staying with the same example, it may be clear that Mr. So & So knowingly shot the Prime Minister, but would we also say that he shot him *intentionally*? Here, I think, we are tempted to say two things at once, both yes and no. This much is clear: he intentionally shot a man he knew to be the Prime Minister, but this seems somehow different from the claim that he shot the Prime Minister intentionally. The difference lies in the fact that *we normally couch our act descriptions in a form that reflects the person's reasons for acting as he did*.[9] Thus if I say that John intentionally shot the Prime Minister, I will be suggesting that his reason (or at least part of his reason) for shooting him was that he was the Prime Minister. Of course, if the facts are clear, this suggestion will be canceled out, and it is always possible to cancel such a suggestion simply by saying all that needs to be said: "John knowingly shot the Prime Minister, not because he was the Prime Minister but because the Prime Minister was his wife's lover."

---

[9]And this accounts for the opacity of act descriptions. If our description is intended to reflect the speaker's reasons for acting as he did, then referring expressions with the same reference cannot be exchanged in a willy-nilly fashion. On the other hand, if the point of our remark is to identify who it is that John shot, then the reference can be transparent.

Suppose, however, that John shot the Prime Minister without realizing that he was the Prime Minister. Here I think we would say that he shot him unknowingly, that is to say, the knowledge that the person he shot was the Prime Minister did not enter into his practical reflection. This, of course, is very different from shooting him by mistake. Mistakes involve error (not just ignorance) ; in particular, they involve some sort of error pertaining to the descriptive content of the practical reasoning. Thus, I can shoot the janitor mistaking him for a thief, or shoot the Prime Minister on the mistaken assumption that he is my wife's lover. In the latter case I might mistakenly shoot the Prime Minister knowing full well that he is the Prime Minister.

Accidents, as Austin has noted, are different animals altogether. If I say that John shot the Prime Minister accidentally, I have then blocked *all* questions concerning his reasons for doing it. In fact, I have done more than this; I have indicated *why* such questions are out of place, but it is surprisingly difficult to specify any of this in detail. Anyway, it is important to notice why accidents differ from mistakes. If John shot the Prime Minister mistakenly, the fact that it was the Prime Minister whom he shot is not relevant to his reasons for shooting him, but he did act from other reasons, and these other reasons can be interrogated.[10]

Thus far this ramble through a child's garden of adverbs has been limited to those that are related to the model as a whole (intentionally, unintentionally, accidentally) and those that concern the descriptive aspects of the model (knowingly, unknowingly, mistakenly). Some other adverbs operate in the region of the prescriptive major. Here I can only consider two contrasting pairs : voluntary-involuntary and willingly-unwillingly are suitable specimens. The general idea is this : certain adverbs indicate the relationship between an agent and the prescriptions he accepts. If a person voluntarily ϕs, then he accepts the prescription to ϕ under no constraint or duress. If he willingly ϕs, then he accepts the prescription to ϕ with a glad heart. And so on. Needless to say, ϕing unintentionally and ϕing involuntarily are very different notions. If a hooligan sticks a gun in my ribs and tells me to hand

---

[10]But even accidents are subject to criticism: "You should have been more careful." But this involves a shift in levels; we do not criticize the person for ϕing, but for comporting himself in such a manner that allowed the ϕing to take place.

over my money, when I do so it is not something that I do unintentionally; but it surely is something that I do involuntarily (and, a fortiori, unwillingly).

Finally, and very quickly, we can notice one adverb that ties into the inferential aspect of the prescriptive model. When we say that a person deliberately øed (in the sense of øing after deliberation) we are simply underscoring the fact that his action was a considered action, in other words, that the reflection marked by the second component took place pretty much explicitly. I have already said that the prescriptive model is not a script for inner dialogue, but for deliberate action it at least approximates this.[11]

VI

Thus far I have been discussing adverbs that modify performances that have actually taken place. Next I want to talk about constructions concerning prospective or envisaged acts. For example, if we speak of what someone intends (or even intended) to do, we are not thereby committing ourselves to saying that it took place. In particular, I want to examine a set of verbs that *accept* (not simply form) infinitives, yielding constructions of the following kind:

intend to ø	want to ø
hope to ø	have to ø
like to ø	need to ø
desire to ø	wish to ø

Excluded from this list are those constructions that admit of an in-order-to expansion. Thus, "John loves to play golf" is in, but "John lives to play golf" is out; for while John may live in order to play golf, he does not love in order to play golf (unless, that is, he is a golf-playing gigolo). There are probably other constructions that should be excluded from the list, but there isn't time to go into any of this in detail. For want of a better name, I shall call this system of verbs "quasi-auxiliaries."

If we pursue the idea that these quasi-auxiliaries govern envisaged or prospective acts, we can see how the prescriptive model can be modified to take them into account. First of all, the third

---

[11] Austin has argued that an action can be done deliberately, but, for all that, not intentionally. Although I cannot go into this, his examples turn upon varying the scope of act descriptions.

component is eliminated altogether—the man who intends to do something need not straightway do it, for the occasion may not be at hand. If we are to abandon the third component, we must throw a monkey wrench in the second component as well. The device for doing this could hardly be more simple: we merely put the descriptive minor in a tense that is future relative to the tense of the antecedent in the prescriptive major. For example, the claim that John intends to shoot the Prime Minister comes to this:

> John accepts the prescription "If the opportunity arises, then shoot the Prime Minister!" and he further believes that the opportunity *will* arise.

The past tense construction is, in a way, more interesting; "John intended to shoot the Prime Minister" comes to this:

> John accept*ed* the prescription "If the opportunity arises, then shoot the Prime Minister," at the same time believing that the opportunity *would* arise.

Because of the tense shift, the reasoning to a prescriptive conclusion does not go through:

> If the opportunity arises, then shoot the Prime Minister.
>
> The opportunity will arise.
> ─────────────────────────────
> ∴ nothing

On the other hand, the person who intends to do something looks forward to the time when the tenses will be aligned, and for this reason *the person who intends to do something believes that he will do it.* In the past tense, the person who intended to do something believed (at that time) that he would do it.

We can get a deeper insight into the character of intend-to constructions by contrasting them with want-to constructions. Provisionally, I shall say that a person wants to do something if and only if:

> (1) He accepts a hypothetical prescription of the form "If the opportunity arises, then do *x*."
>
> (2) Without, either:
>
>   (a) having any settled belief that the opportunity will arise, or
>
>   (b) taking into account every overriding demand.

The two qualifications mark two ways that wants differ from intentions. The first qualification brings out this difference: a person can want to do something without having any firm belief that he will do it, but, as we have seen, if he intends to do it, he does firmly believe that he will do it.

The second qualification is more interesting. A person may want to do something but still not do it when the occasion presents itself because he gives precedence to some other prescription. This is logically possible because wants involve a qualified commitment to a prescription, and this qualified commitment can remain in force *at the very same time* that we are not doing what we want to do. Intentions are different. A person who intends to do something believes that nothing overrides his commitment. Of course, he may be mistaken (or self-deceived) on both counts, but when he becomes aware of his mistakes he will *abandon* his intention in precisely a fashion that he need not abandon his wants or desires. This may sound like too strong a claim, but notice that both of the following remarks are aberrant:

> I intend to do it, but I won't do it because I now see that the opportunity will not arise.

> I intend to do it, but I won't do it because I have other more important things to do.

In order to restore sense to these remarks, we have to cast the verb in the past tense to leave open the possibility that the intention is no longer operative.[12]

If we move further away from the strong commitment involved in intentions, we come to wishes and even idle wishes. In an idle wish I accept a prescription in full knowledge that I will never act upon it. I may idly wish to insult the chancellor to his face, knowing full well that such doings are ruled out by demands of prudence. Or, I may idly wish to issue a papal encyclical, recognizing that my chances for the needed preferment are absolutely nil. The commitment of an idle wish is pretty thin, but still there is some commitment involved; what I idly wish to do is something I'd intend to do in some other possible world.

VII

Before concluding, I shall say some general things about purposes and motives. One striking feature of the prescriptive model,

---

[12]In most cases, not doing what we want to do is a sign of strength of character; not doing what we intend to do is a sign of weakness of the will.

as it now stands, is that it gives no account of purposes. In its present form, the middle component does not provide a way of reflecting the fact that we sometimes do one thing in order to accomplish something else (or, somewhat differently, that we do one thing *as a part* of doing something larger). To accommodate these notions we will have to expand the model to include instrumental (and mereological) premises. This is hardly a routine undertaking, and for my own part I am willing to wait until logicians have completed their labors before exploring matters further.

In saying that the prescriptive model as it now stands is seriously incomplete, I am not trying to disarm the reader with my candor. The incompleteness is serious. In particular, without a much richer account of the structure of practical reasoning, we cannot give an adequate account of the variable scope (or accordion character) of human actions. It is now a commonplace that the very same performance can be truly described by act descriptions differing in temporal stretch, differing in generality, or (seemingly) differing in just being different. My idea now is that different act descriptions are possible in virtue of the fact that the line of practical reasoning can be sliced by a description at different points. Crudely, we can imagine a segment of practical reflection having the following form:

(G) ϕ !

In order to ϕ, θ !

∴ θ !

If our act description cuts the practical reasoning above the instrumental premise, we will then say that Mr. So & So ϕed; if it cuts it below this premise, we will say that he θed. Thus we can say that Brutus stabbed Caesar and also that he killed Caesar. We might also recognize the connection between these two claims through understanding their respective roles in the practical reasoning. In other words, we might realize that Brutus stabbed Caesar *in order* to kill him. It is, however, the relationship within the pracical reasoning that counts here; with a sufficiently morbid imagination, we could think of a case where someone kills a person in order to stab him.

In considering motives, we first must see that motives and purposes are different. I may know, for example, that a person is climbing the trellis in order to dance on the roof, but I may be completely in the dark about his motives for dancing on the roof. Furthermore, we often talk about purposes where talk about motives seems out of place. When I discover that the man is climbing the trellis in order to dance on the roof, I do not ask about his motive for climbing the trellis. Talk about motives centers on what he is out to accomplish, not on the means he uses to bring it off. This suggests that motives concern the ultimate commitment (or commitments) that stand at the beginning of practical reflection. Thus a person's motive for dancing on the roof might be that he wants to show off. Thus he starts out from the prescriptive major "Show off!" Then, through a process of instrumental reflection, he settles upon what he sees to be the best way to accomplish this: he will dance on the roof.

Once more, an act description may cut this pattern of reflection at different points. In response to the question "What is he doing?" we might answer:

Dancing on the roof.
Making a display of himself.
Showing off.

Again, we can relate these claims in a manner that reflects their role in his practical reasoning: he is dancing on the roof *in order to* make a display of himself, and he is making a display of himself because he *wants to* show off. Of course, he might have some further reason for wanting to show off, and this would reveal that we have yet to penetrate his motives fully. Then again, his acceptance of the prescription "Show off!" might be the end of the line, and further talk about motives simply would be otiose.

Of course, when reasons (in the sense of a practical premise for action) give out, we may still press on and ask about the *causes* that led to the acceptance of the practical premises. A person might want to show off because of an inferiority complex, but it would be an odd context where a person would act in this way as the result of accepting the practical premise "Manifest the symptoms of a person with an inferiority complex!" The best example I can think of where a person might act under this practical premise is the case of a person *pretending* to have an inferiority complex. An inferiority complex involves the tendency to accept certain prescriptions in given circumstances, but "Manifest the symptoms of a person with an inferiority complex!" is not among them. A similar remark holds for terms describing character traits, but this is not the place to examine this in detail.

VIII

The major weakness of the prescriptive model as it has thus far been developed is in the structure of the practical reasoning embedded as its middle component. It certainly must be expanded to include instrumental and mereological premises, and beyond this its simple linear form must be replaced by a branching structure that reflects the plurality of reasons that can bear upon a single action. Furthermore, I think that the acceptance of a categorical prescription straightway issues into action only when the action prescribed involves a skill or capacity possessed by the agent. Otherwise, the practical reflection continues until it terminates either (1) in a prescription that the person can straightway perform, or (2) in a prescription that the person thinks he will be able to perform some time in the future, or (3) in a simple blockage. In the first case we get an action; in the second, an intention; and in the third, a want or wish (which may perish in the face of the blockage).

In sum, then, a fully developed treatment of the middle component of the prescriptive model will reveal structures of argument that I have hardly touched upon. Nonetheless, even in its nascent form the prescriptive model has two general features that create a presumption in its favor. One fact about statements describing human actions is that they admit of questions concerning a person's *reasons* for doing what he has done, where reasons are somehow thought to be different from causes. The model accounts for this datum in an entirely natural way by relating it to the connection between a premise and a conclusion. Another fact about statements describing human actions is that they seem to be somehow directional or teleological. On the prescriptive model this feature is captured quite simply through the use of prescriptions, for prescriptions are paradigms of constructions with a forward-looking reference. So however incomplete (or faulty) my account of this model might be, there is at least some reason to believe that the general approach is not entirely misguided.

Seeing and Justification

FRED I. DRETSKE

Our acquisition of knowledge by visual means is incremental in character. The increments in question, those pieces of information we acquire by seeing that something is the case, are systematically reflected in the way we describe our visual achievements. A proper appreciation of the magnitude of these increments, if I may use the word "magnitude" in this respect, is of first importance to the philosophy of perception. Without it we are in the position of a man who attempts to determine how fast he can run by examining the point at which he stops running. Such a person needs to be told that the pertinent variable here is not where he stopped running, not even where he started running, but the distance between these two points. By analogy, what is relevant in the philosophy of perception, especially its epistemology, is not the information we possess at the finish line, so to speak, but the increment of information we acquired in getting there.

It should be understood at the outset that I am not concerned with what has been called the nonpropositional sense of seeing. That is to say, I am not interested, except incidentally, with a person's seeing a clear liquid; rather, I am concerned with his seeing that the liquid is clear. An individual, *S*, might easily see a liquid (which was clear) without seeing that it was clear—without even seeing that it was a liquid. It is these latter, essentially epistemic, achievements with which this paper is concerned. I shall, therefore, concentrate on those perceptual reports that embody a factive nominal although I do not wish to suggest by this that these are the only grammatical constructions which are relevant to the inquiry.

Frequently, but certainly not in every case, a statement involving the construction "see that" tells us, not only *what* someone knows, or has found, to be the case, but also *how* he knows, or has found, it to be the case. If I tell you that I stopped because I could see that the road was blocked, it is fairly clear, I think, that the latter clause tells you not only what I discovered (that the road was blocked) but how I discovered it (I *saw* that it was blocked). One of our standard responses to the query "How do you know?" is a statement about what we have seen, or can see, to be the case, and these responses describe *the manner* in which we have come to know. They tell us that the knowledge was acquired in some essentially *visual* manner. There are other settings, however, in which this visual element is absent. For instance, I might remark mid-way through a tedious lecture that I can see why my friend declined the invitation to attend or, perhaps, can see that the speaker has never read Aristotle. I needn't have my eyes open to see these things. In expressing myself in this way I am doing little more than telling you what I have come to realize; I certainly am not attempting to describe the manner in which I achieved this realization. There are countless examples of this "nonvisual" seeing. Nonetheless, I think it obvious that in a vast number of situations the "seeing that" locution has the additional force of indicating *the manner* in which we have discovered something, and it is these situations that are crucial to the epistemology of perception. For in such settings, directly or indirectly justificatory in nature, to say of someone that he saw that so-and-so was the case is to tell not only what he knows but how he knows it. It is this particular class of situations to which the remainder of my paper is addressed.

If I may be permitted the use of an overidealized schema for the moment, the point I am after can be put as follows: when the statement "S sees (or can see) that the b is P" is designed to tell not only what S knows (or realizes) but also how he knows it, then such a statement *only* tells us how S knows that the b is P. It does *not* tell us how he knows that it is a b which is P. When George, in response to a query about how he knows that the flowers are wilted, replies that he can see that they are wilted, George has not told us how he knows that they are flowers (which he sees to be wilted). His statement certainly implies that he has identified the flowers as flowers, but it does not tell us how he arrived at this identification. In particular, his statement does not tell us that he does, or even *can,* see that they are flowers. George can know that the flowers are wilted by virtue of seeing that they are wilted without seeing, without even being able to see, that they are flowers which are wilted.

Suppose you convince yourself that a certain liquid in a bottle is indeed wine (and not just fruit juice or colored water) by tasting it. You then remark, halfway through the evening, that you can see that the wine is almost gone. Does this entail that you are able, or think yourself able, to see that the liquid in the bottle is wine? Of course not. You know it is wine by having tasted it, and you know that it (the wine) is almost gone because you can see that it is almost gone. One can see that the *b* is *P* without being able to see that it is *b* (or a *b*) which is *P*. This is why one can see that the widow is dressed in black without being able to see that it is a widow (who is) dressed in black.

This point may strike some people as extremely trivial. Perhaps it is. Nonetheless, I think it is of the utmost importance. For if we are going to concern ourselves with the validity (justificatory adequacy) of our commonsense perceptual claims, as philosophers are wont to do, then we must be quite clear as to what is and what is not being claimed in our ordinary perceptual reports. And if what I have just suggested is true, then we must be extremely careful not to confuse seeing that the flower is wilted with seeing that it is a wilted flower. If we treat these two achievements as a single achievement described in alternative ways, we will mistakenly suppose that if someone cannot see that something is a wilted flower, neither can he see that the flower is wilted. And this is simply not true. Nor, for the same reasons, is it true that I cannot see that this is a tomato (a real tomato) simply because I cannot (let us say) distinguish between a real tomato and an hallucinatory figment of my own imagination on purely visual grounds, for, as I shall attempt to show, these are also two quite different visual achievements.

To change the example slightly, why is it that someone may truly say, "I can see that the water is boiling," but not be able to truly say, in the same set of circumstances, "I can see that this is boiling water"? The reason has already been suggested. When we take the word "water" out of the predicate position (this is boiling water) and transfer it to the subject position (this water is boiling), we thereby alter what it is we are claiming to have achieved *visually*. When I assert, "I can see that the water (or this water) is boiling," I am in effect telling you that I know several things, but, and this is the important point, I am only telling you *how* I know one of these things. I am telling you that I have identified this as water (but I am *not* telling you how I arrived at this identification) and I am telling you that I know that it is boiling (and I *am* telling you how I know this: I can *see* that it is boiling). If, then, we put the word "water" in the predicate position, "I can see that this is boiling water" (without excessive stress on either the word "water" or the word "boiling"), I am still telling you that I know several things, both that this is water and that this is boiling, but now I am telling you *how* I know *both* of these things—I can *see* that it is boiling water. And this simple change makes all the difference. For I may, under certain circumstances, be able to see that the liquid (which I have *already* identified, on independent grounds, as water) is boiling without being able to see that the liquid is water. The fact that we can, generally speaking, know that something is water in ways other than, or supplementary to, seeing that it is water is what makes it possible to see that the water is boiling without being able to see that it is boiling water.

In many instances, of course, we can see not only that the *b* is *P,* but that it is indeed a *b* which is *P.* I can see not only that the dog is limping, but that it is a dog which is limping. How do I know that the dog is limping? I can see that it is limping. How do I know that it is a dog which is limping? I can see that it is a dog. But the point I am pressing is that our capacity to reply in this last way is not essentially involved in our ability to see that the dog is limping. I might only know that it is a dog because a committee of canine experts informed me that it was. Up to this time I had never seen a dog nor a picture of a dog. Being completely ignorant of dogs and what they look like, I may be unable to see whether anything, much less this particular thing, is a dog or not. Yet, this does not prevent me from seeing that this dog is limping. In this case I know that the dog is limping because I can see that it is; and I know it is a dog because they told me it was (and they ought to know).

Generally speaking, then, we must distinguish two pieces of information that are conveyed by an epistemic perceptual report. First, it tells us that the percipient knows something and it tells us what it is he knows: that *b* is *P.* Secondly, it tells us how *part* of this information was acquired; and it is this part, this increment in knowledge, which is the essence of the visual achievement. I say this is the essence of the visual achievement because it is only this increment in information that the perceptual report describes as having been acquired by distinctively *visual* means. The increment in knowledge which a perceptual report represents the percipient as having bridged by visual means is that increment *between* the information that this is a *b* and the information that this *b* is *P*. We are told how the percipient got from one point to the other, but on the question of how he arrived at the starting point, how he might justify a claim to be at that starting point, the perceptual report itself is completely silent.

An important negative principle emerges from this discussion. Suppose that something cannot be a *P* unless it is also *Q*. Suppose, furthermore, that *Q* is the sort of feature or characteristic which we cannot, for some special reason, see that something possesses. With only this much information some philosophers might be tempted to conclude that, strictly speaking, one can never see that anything is *P*. For to see that anything is *P* one must be in a position to see that it has those properties without which it could not be *P* and since, by hypothesis, we cannot see that anything is *Q*, neither can we (strictly speaking) see that anything is *P* (although we might conclude that it was *P* on a diversity of other grounds). The previous discussion has shown us why this conclusion must be rejected. It must be rejected because if *S* sees that the *b* is *P*, where something's being a *b* also involves its being *Q*, then the unobservability of *Q* is, strictly speaking, irrelevant to whether *S* can see that the *b* is *P*. It is irrelevant because the possession of *Q* by what *S* sees is *not* embodied in that increment of information which *S*'s statement depicts him as bridging by visual means; it is not part of that information which *S* acquired by seeing that something was so. A few examples may help to clarify this further.

To use philosophical jargon, we all know that tomatoes are physical objects and as such possess properties not possessed by reflections, mental images, and so on. That is to say, tomatoes have mass and an internal structure; they persist through time, and they can be touched, squeezed, tasted, smelled, and, finally, eaten—not only by ourselves but by others as well. Call these properties $Q_1 \ldots Q_n$. Now if one is sceptical of our ability to see, in some straightforward visual sense of this term, that anything has the property Q_i (for any "i"), one might (mistakenly) become sceptical of our ability to see that anything is a tomato. Consider, however, the following perceptual claim: "S can see that this piece of fruit is a tomato." I think there is little question but that something's being a piece of fruit *also* involves its having the properties $Q_1 \ldots Q_n$; a piece of fruit has mass, an internal structure; it persists through time, and it can be touched, squeezed, tasted, smelled, and, finally, eaten—not only by ourselves but by others as well. And what this perceptual report describes S as having found out by visual means is that *the piece of fruit* was a tomato; it does not describe him as having discovered, by any distinctively visual means, that it was a piece of fruit. Hence, the perceptual report is conspicuously silent on the matter of how S found out that what he was seeing possessed the properties $Q_1 \ldots Q_n$. It certainly does not imply that S could see that something was Q_1 or Q_2 or Q_n. Therefore, with respect to this particular perceptual claim, questions of wax imitations, reflections, or hallucinations are totally irrelevant since there is nothing in S's achievement, as so described, which implies that he ruled out, or was capable of ruling out, these possibilities on any sort of visual grounds.

When a person makes a claim, such as the one described above, he could, I suppose, be hallucinating. A mistake such as this might occur. But a mistake of this sort, or the possibility of such a mistake, shows nothing about whether S *can* see what he alleges himself to have seen. The possibility of such mistakes shows something about S's total information-gathering resources. If S is afflicted with such visual hallucinations, it shows (perhaps) that S cannot, on visual grounds alone, determine whether what he sees is a real piece of fruit or not. But since his perceptual report (I can see that this piece of fruit is a tomato) does not depict him as having found out, or even being able to find out, on purely visual grounds that what he is seeing is a real piece of fruit, the *possibility* of such delusions is not even relevant to what S claims to have done.

Even when we take such minimally committed subject expressions as the demonstrative pronouns (unaccompanied by a sortal) we find the same feature present. When I say that I can see that *this* is a tomato, I am telling you how I know that it (this thing to which I direct your attention, this thing to which your attention can be directed by the simple use of a demonstrative with, perhaps, some appropriate gesture) is a tomato. I am not telling you how I know that what I see to be a tomato has those features which allow me to direct your attention to it in this simple demonstrative way. That is, I am not telling you how I know that what I take to be a tomato is not simply a delusory figment of my own imagination, or how I know that it is something that you and other people can also see. This is information which is already embodied in my use of a simple demonstrative to refer to what I see; it is not something which I describe myself as having discovered by seeing that it was so. Hence, the question of visual hallucination and other sorts of gross delusion (involving what have been called "existential mistakes") are not even relevant to whether I can see that this is a tomato, for such a report does not commit me to being able to see that this is a *real* tomato when "*real* tomato" is meant to contrast with "an hallucinatory figment of my own imagination." But, of course, I must see that it is a real tomato if this is understood as contrasting with "a wax imitation."

We cannot ask of a term or phrase, in isolation, whether it represents or expresses an observable feature of things or not. For we cannot answer this question until we know *what it is* that is observed to have this feature, what increment in information it is of which this term or phrase expresses the terminus. And we cannot discover this until we look at the specific perceptual claims that embody a use of this term or phrase. Suppose, for instance, that we can construct robots that are visually indistinguishable from real people (externally). Now what shall we say about the predicate "is embarrassed"? Is it, as they say, an observational predicate or not? If we assume that mechanical robots are not really embarrassed (although they may look as though they are), it may seem that since, by hypothesis, we cannot *see* whether something is a real person or one of our remarkable robots, neither can we *see* whether something is really embarrassed. But this is simply false. There is nothing to prevent us from seeing that *our wife, son,* or *friend* is embarrassed (unless, of course, a robot happened to be one of our friends). In these cases the possibility that we are seeing a robot, although it is ruled out, is not said to be ruled out on *visual* grounds. The increment here is (or may be) sufficiently small to bridge by visual means alone even though we are unable to tell, by visual means alone, whether what we are seeing is the sort of thing that *could* be embarrassed.

There are, admittedly, a good many objects of the verb "to see" that do not exemplify the overidealized grammatical pattern with which I have been working. I do not have the time to discuss all the subtleties, but I think a few examples will illustrate that my analysis is not restricted to a few peculiar cases. Consider the statement "I can see that the pencil is on the table." Here we are being told, not how the speaker knows that it is a pencil which is on the table, not how he knows that it is a table, but simply how he knows that the one is *on* the other. No doubt we would expect anyone making such a report to be able to see whether it was a pencil on the table and see whether it was a table that the pencil was on, but (and this is the point) his inability to do so is quite irrelevant to whether he can see that the pencil is on the table.

It should be noticed, in passing, that a statement of the form "He saw the pencil on the table" or "He saw the table with the pencil on it," since they do not tell us *how* he discovered, or even *whether* he discovered, that there was a pencil on a table, are quite immune to epistemological objections. He need not be in a position to see that there is a pencil on the table, or that the pencil is on a table, to see the pencil which is on the table. Hence, sceptical quibbles about whether he is able to identify the pencil as a pencil, the table as a table, or justify the claim that the one is on the other, are quite irrelevant to whether he saw the pencil (which was) on the table.

Consider, finally, a typical "existential" clause. Suppose our companion sees that there is a bug in his soup and remarks upon it. I should naturally suppose that my companion not only saw that there was a bug in his soup, but could also see that it was *his soup* that the bug was in. But although I might naturally suppose this, his perceptual report itself is noncommittal in this respect. He has told us how he discovered that there was a bug in his soup; he has not told us how he discovered, how he knows, that there is some soup, his soup, or some real soup, which the bug is in. This plateau of information is presupposed by his perceptual report. If we are interested in determining whether he can really see what he purports to see, the question to ask is not "Can he really distinguish this experience from an hallucinatory one?" but, rather, "Given that it is *his soup* which he is seeing, is he in a position to tell, on visual grounds alone, whether there is a bug in it?"

There are countless subtleties on this basic theme. To take the last example, we should notice that it is quite a different thing to "see that there is a bug in your soup" than it is to "see that it is a bug that is in your soup." For the latter statement tells us *only* how the percipient identified *what was in his soup* as a bug rather than, say, a noodle or a mushroom; the former statement tells us, in addition, how the percipient discovered that *there was something* in his soup. For example, it would be easier for a person given over to eidetic imagery of a rather vivid sort (mental images projected onto the normal surroundings) to see that it was a bug that was in his soup than it would be for him to see that there was a bug in his soup. The former claim does not tell us how he knows that he is seeing *something in his soup* while the latter claim does tell us this.

In my efforts to make a point, I may have created a misleading impression. I certainly do not wish to dispute that people make mistakes, and that sometimes they do not know that which their perceptual claims imply they know. I only wish to urge that many of these mistakes are irrelevant to a proper epistemological evaluation of whether people possess the talent to discover, and hence know, that something is so in virtue of seeing that it is so. Consider the following:

> *S* :   The captain is very young indeed.
> *R* :   What makes you say that?
> *S* :   I can see that he is; just look at him!
> *R* :   That is the porter, not the captain.
> *S* :   Oh, my wife told me he was the captain.

If we expand *S*'s second statement into the perceptual claim "I can see that the captain is a very young man" we might want to ask whether this statement is true or false. In one respect it is clearly false; the captain is not (let us say) a very young man, and so *S* could scarcely be right in saying that he sees that he is very young. Still, the fact remains that the increment in knowledge which *S* alleges himself to have acquired by visual means *is* an increment which he can easily bridge and, in the present case, is actually bridging with respect to that fellow over there (the porter). This sort of mistake has no bearing on whether *S* can see whether a man is young or not; it simply shows that in this particular case the man he saw to be young was not who he thought he was. But since he never said that he could see that *that* man was the captain (although he might have believed he could see this), his mistake does not infect that portion of his claim which was essentially visual. This kind of mistake is certainly of interest to epistemology, but not to the epistemology of perception —*visual* perception. Consider another case:

S :   I see that this water is frozen already.

R :   That is glass, not water.

S :   Oh really! Why is there glass in this tray and water in all the rest?

In this case we might want to say that S's perceptual claim is a nonstarter. His mistake is real enough, but, once again, this kind of mistake does not reflect adversely on his capacity to achieve visually what he purports to have achieved visually. S is quite able to see, in such circumstances as now prevail, whether water is frozen or not. He is quite able to bridge the gap he thinks he is bridging (and says he is bridging)—the gap between "this is water" and "this water is frozen." He is simply not starting from where he thinks he is starting. But the responsibility for being at the correct starting point is not a responsibility that rests solely, or even primarily, on his sense of sight. The responsibility rests with his total information-gathering resources: his intellect, memory, powers of inference, and other senses. To suppose that such mistakes show something about the epistemological inadequacy of his (or our) *visual* powers is like concluding that our center forward is inadequate because, and only because, our team keeps losing.

I have not addressed myself to the question of whether those bits (increments) of information which our perceptual reports *do* imply were acquired by visual means can, in fact, be acquired on distinctively visual grounds alone, whether we can *justifiably* go from "this is water" to "this water is frozen" on visual grounds alone as the locution "sees that the water is frozen" would suggest. This is another question entirely. I think it can be answered (affirmatively) to the satisfaction of a sceptic, but it would require a much longer paper. All I have been attempting to argue here is that questions of the sort "Couldn't it be glass?" or "Might it not be a clever imitation?" are irrelevant to the question of whether we *can* see that water is frozen and that the piece of fruit is a tomato. And, more significantly, the query "Couldn't you be hallucinating?" is irrelevant to whether I can see that this or that is a table, pencil, or my own left hand in a straightforward visual manner.

One final caution about the completeness of my argument. I have concentrated heavily on first person, present tense reports of what is seen. Further complications arise when we move to third person reports and past tense statements. When I say of S that he saw that the water was frozen, I certainly suggest that he knew that it was water that was frozen, but we occasionally take considerable liberties with this associated "suggestion." He may *not* have known it was water; he may only have identified is as a liquid of some sort. Still, even knowing this, I may say that he saw that the water was frozen. Whether I say this or not will depend on several factors, one of the most important being the ease with which my listeners are able to identify what it is that S saw to be frozen. Comparable flexibility is available in first person reports when they are in the past tense. But I am convinced that an extended analysis of this variability will only tend to support the point I have been urging throughout this paper: that a vast number of, perhaps all, perceptual reports which tell us how a person discovered something tell us only how he discovered a small piece of that information which the perceptual report implies that he possesses. And to the question of whether we can acquire these pieces of information in the manner described, many of the traditional sceptical considerations are simply irrelevant.

Comments

PHILIP HUGLY

Professor Dretske's main positive thesis concerns the relation between perception and knowledge implied in what he calls our commonsense perceptual claims. In connection with his analysis of this relation he says,

> . . . I think [my main point] is of the utmost importance. For if we are going to concern ourselves with the validity . . . of our commonsense perceptual claims, as philosophers are wont to do, then we must be quite clear as to what is and what is not being claimed in our ordinary perceptual reports.

The philosophers Dretske has in mind are those who have raised what seem to be *sceptical* questions about our common knowledge. Thus he attributes special importance to his analysis of our commonsense perceptual claims in terms of its relation to the sceptical considerations of traditional epistemology. My comments will be mainly concerned with this relation, and I will follow Dretske in paying particular attention to the traditional appeal to the hallucination possibility.

I

The main types of commonsense perceptual claims dealt with by Dretske are identifications and characterizations. He says that the hallucination possibility is irrelevant to such claims. Near the end of his paper he suggests that this possibility may be irrelevant to all of our commonsense perceptual claims. I will begin with a quick review of some of the difficulties that seem to stand in the way of a straightforward assessment of these ideas.

The first difficulty is that Dretske never tells us anything about that appeal to the hallucination possibility which transforms it into a "traditional sceptical consideration." Instead he only cites such sentences as "Couldn't you be hallucinating?" But we do not use such sentences as this *only* in philosophy. We also use such sentences in ordinary epistemic situations.

The fact is, I think, that a great many commonsense claims are, in certain circumstances (and quite apart from any philosophical reflection), open to doubts based on the hallucination possibility. From our commonsense point of view, of course, the circumstances must either be known or reasonably suspected to be quite special before we can properly appeal to this possibility by way of raising a doubt. And most of the situations within which we ordinarily find ourselves neither contain nor can reasonably be thought to contain circumstances of the sort required to legitimize appeal to this possibility. But this in no way implies that the number of claims which *in one situation or another* would be open to the hallucination doubt is small. *Any* claim which *could* be made in a situation in which the hallucination possibility could be appealed to in raising doubts will be a claim that is *open* to the hallucination doubt.

Consider, for example, the following claim and perceptual basis report: "There is a robin in the oak"; "I can see that there is a robin in the oak." Now in most situations in which one might make that claim on that basis there would be no question raised at all. In *some* situations a question might arise as to whether the person really knows that it is a *robin* in the oak. And here a person might answer by saying that he knows robins when he sees them or that he can tell it is a robin because he can see that it has a red breast, etc. And in *some* situations we might question the person's claim by raising the possibility that he is hallucinating. For example, suppose that he has said that there is a robin in the oak and that he can see that there is one there. I look at the tree very carefully and cannot see any bird whatsoever in the tree. Further, I have reason to believe that he has recently been experimenting with drugs that sometimes have hallucinatory side effects. So I say to him: "I can't see any bird there at all—maybe you're just hallucinating one." Now suppose that he in fact had been taking those drugs and that he looked at me as I spoke to him and that when he looked back up to the tree he could no longer see any bird there. Now he is in doubt. He is unable either definitely to rule out this possibility *or* establish that he had suffered an hallucination. Now he just shakes his head and says: "I don't know whether there was a robin there or not. I might have been hallucinating. I just don't know."

Now this commonsense perceptual claim would most often be made in circumstances in which no one would think of worrying about hallucination. In most situations we have no reason for thinking that a person is hallucinating and would find it unreasonable to try to raise a doubt by appealing to that possibility. But circumstances could exist in which it would simply be commonsense to worry about that possibility. And if, in those circumstances, the possibility could not be ruled out then that claim would have to be abandoned or at least reduced to an expression of belief. And there are, of course, a huge number of such claims.

Further, in the case described, there was no hint of philosophy. The case was one in which the hallucination possibility was appealed to in an ordinary or commonsense way—not in a philosophical way.

Thus I am led to think that the generalization of Dretske's view must be wrong as regards *ordinary* appeals to the hallucination possibility. There are many commonsense perceptual claims to which the hallucination possibility is not "simply irrelevant." Dretske's view, however, might not be wrong as regards *philosophical* appeals to this possibility. Perhaps all philosophical appeals are "simply irrelevant" to our commonsense claims. But this crucial distinction is not drawn, and it is thus very difficult to decide whether and to what degree what Dretske says is or is not true.

Next, when we turn from "existential" claims such as "I see that there is a robin in the oak" to Dretske's main examples of straightforward identificatory and characterizational claims we run into an analogous difficulty. Has he shown that *philosophical* appeals to the hallucination possibility are irrelevant to such claims? Or has he shown only that *ordinary* appeals to this possibility are irrelevant to such claims? Apart from a discussion of the distinction it is very hard to tell. My belief is that he argues only the irrelevance of the ordinary appeal. Now suppose that his claim of irrelevance is correct in this connection. What would this show us about the force of the philosophical appeal to this possibility? Again it is very hard to tell. Everything would depend on how Dretske would bridge the gap between the ordinary and the philosophical appeals. My guess is that his arguments implicitly rely on a linking premise to the effect that if a commonsense claim cannot be challenged by an ordinary appeal to the hallucination possibility then no claim of its form can be challenged by any type of appeal to that possibility.

If this conjecture is correct then we could formulate Dretske's general method as follows: One first shows that commonsense claims with a certain form (e.g., identifications with a "that" clause) are, in virtue of that form, immune to challenge by ordinary appeals to the hallucination possibility. Second, one generalizes this result through the previously mentioned sort of premise. If this is his method, then it clearly has some substantial limitations, for as noted above there are types of commonsense perceptual claims that *can* be directly challenged by ordinary appeals to the hallucination possibility, and if there are such claims then the linking premise becomes inoperative and the possibility remains that the generally undermining sceptical appeal to the hallucination possibility may also be in order.

I have placed a great deal of weight on the idea that we can distinguish between ordinary and philosophical appeals to the hallucination possibility. It seems plain to me that there is some difference here, but this does not mean it is easy to set out and describe the difference. I will now try to indicate the kind of difference I see. My account will be both rough and intuitive. To do the job correctly would require a degree of detailed analytic understanding that would take many pages for its presentation and that, in any case, I do not yet possess. Further, I will not discuss all of the ways in which the difference I am concerned with might be brought out. Instead I will concentrate on bringing out the difference as it appears when epistemologists cast their thoughts in the form of philosophical certainty inquiries.[1]

1. The epistemologist's basic subject matter is our *common* (shared and unspecialized) knowledge of ordinary public objects. His initial reflection on this dimension of our common knowledge discloses the following two propositions as being of fundamental importance: (i) There exist a great many public objects, the most important of which are physical or material wholes. (ii) We see

---

[1]Much of what I say in the following ten paragraphs has been suggested to me by the work of Professor Thompson Clarke of the Berkeley philosophy department. I am not suggesting, however, that what I say in these sections is at all an adequate reflection of his work.

public objects—most importantly those which are physical or material wholes such as tables and chairs—but also many which are not such wholes, e.g., explosions, shadows, flashes, etc.

2. A metaphysician or conceptual analyst (for example, P. F. Strawson in his book *Individuals*[2]) would construe these two propositions as propositions that express certain fundamental facts about our *conceptual* apparatus. A philosopher of this type would speak about how these propositions tell us something important about how we *think* or *conceive* of ourselves and the world around us. He would not look upon these propositions as expressing anything about our *beliefs*. Even a speculative metaphysician who rejected these propositions would not reject them as expressing false or unsubstantiated *beliefs*. An epistemologist, on the other hand, would think about these propositions in terms of "what we believe." He does this by conceptualizing these propositions in *epistemic* terms. He represents the first proposition as something we *know* and represents the second proposition as providing *grounds* for this knowledge. "We know that there exist public, physical objects because we can see and touch them."

3. Neither of these propositions directly enters into our ordinary claims. We do not, in common life, ever try to establish the general claim that there exist physical things. Rather, we work against a background in which the existence of public, physical things is unquestioned (except in particular cases). Our explicit claims are only about the existence of this or that particular item. It is a matter of determining whether or not some *place* identified in connection with a whole "matrix" of physical items is "filled" by some further physical item.

4. Thus the epistemologist sees these propositions as expressing our implicit and implied beliefs. His epistemic characterization of these propositions takes the following, well-known form: "We all believe (it is part of commonsense to believe) that we can know that there exist public, physical objects and that we can know there are such objects because we can see, touch, and otherwise perceive them." By casting these basic propositions in epistemic terms—terms whose very meaning is essentially connected with our *activities* of *making* and *investigating* claims to knowl-

---

[2] (London, 1959). I have in mind his work in chapter I of this book, especially the first part of that chapter and his remarks on p. 30 about public points of reference.

edge and certainty—the epistemologist prepares the way for his certainty inquiry as an investigation of our "underlying beliefs."

5. Given this general perspective the epistemologist proceeds to his specific inquiry by working with some *paradigmatically normal* perceptual situation, that is, a situation which can be used both as an example and as a test case because it is paradigmatically normal ("best possible"). The situation might be that of himself holding and looking at some sheets of paper (Descartes[3]) or of being before a table (Russell[4]) or a tomato (Price[5]). Thus, for example, I might turn to a nearby object and say, "Now I surely *know* there is a typewriter here for I can see it here before me now." Now once one has inserted the conceptual structure of making a claim and providing a basis, one is committed by the nature of that structure to an investigation. There is nothing philosophical about this commitment. As Austin pointed out in connection with ordinary cases, once one has said, "I know," then one is open to the question "How do you know?" and committed to defending what one says against objections.[6] In this case the fact that the claim is existential and that the grounds were perceptual makes the possibility of *delusive* perception a natural objection. Thus the philosopher may raise to himself the possibility that he is only hallucinating. Here the crucial fact is that he does not raise this possibility in connection with any of the sorts of factors that would ordinarily lead us to consider it seriously. He does not imagine that other people do not see the typewriter or that he has been taking drugs or anything of that sort. The most he will do is remind himself that people do sometimes hallucinate and that, of course, is not a *reason* for thinking one is here and now hallucinating. Further, the epistemologist *could not* raise this possibility in connection with any of the usual special factors, for if he did then his situation would cease to be paradigmatically normal and thus would lose its power of disclosing any *general* truth. (The generalization of the epistemologist's insights is not provided through an inductive enumeration of

[3]Descartes, *Meditations on First Philosophy,* Meditation I.

[4]Bertrand Russell, *The Problems of Philosophy* (New York, 1959; first published in 1912), pp. 7–9.

[5]H. H. Price, *Perception* (London, 1932), p. 3.

[6]J. L. Austin, "Other Minds," reprinted in *Philosophical Papers* (London, 1961), pp. 45–46.

many cases but rather is provided by the paradigmatic nature of the one case with which he works.)

6. Thus, within the structure of his inquiry the epistemologist will find himself required to consider, for example, the hallucination possibility quite apart from any special reason for thinking that he may actually be hallucinating. He is thereby forced to make this possibility real to himself apart from any such reason. This is the single most difficult part of his inquiry. He must see how he could here and now be hallucinating. To succeed in this is to realize how one could have just this perceptual experience and yet be hallucinating. And so, once one realizes how this is possible, one also realizes that there are no "certain marks" and that one cannot, here and now, be certain that there is, for example, a typewriter present. This represents the *epistemic* or *sceptical* upshot of the hallucination inquiry.

7. The next move in this inquiry is for the epistemologist to ask himself, "What then can I be certain of?" and the only answer available is "All I can now be certain of is that I now see just those colors and shapes." This is the *perceptual* upshot of the hallucination inquiry. It expresses the sense-datum thesis of perception.

8. It is essential to see that this sense-datum thesis is not *presupposed* by this inquiry but rather is a *result* of this inquiry. Once this result is attained it is then possible to invoke the argument from *illusion* to prove that what one here sees is a private and not a public item. This "argument" attains its aim in basically the following way: "Now fix your attention on those colors and shapes about which alone you are now certain. Notice that as you move around the typewriter those colors and shapes change. Notice also that no one else would at any moment see just that distribution of colors and shapes that you see at this moment."

9. Thus the hallucination inquiry (a particular instance of what we might call "the argument from delusion") brings us to fix our attention on the "common-sensuous element" in perception by forcing us to consider seriously the possibility that we are hallucinating. The argument from illusion consists in a subsidiary set of instructions that, when followed, shows us that this "common-sensuous element" we have *already* identified is private. At this point we reach the full significance of the philosophical appeal to the hallucination possibility. It (a) throws *doubt* upon

the first proposition (that there exist public, physical items and that we can know this) and (b) entirely *rejects* the second proposition (that we see public items). (That many epistemologists decide to reserve the *expression* "see" or at least "indirectly see" for use in material object *sentences* does not conflict with the idea that the second proposition is entirely rejected.)

10. Finally, I would suggest that the philosophical appeal to the hallucination possibility differs from our ordinary appeal to that possibility in these two ways: First, the possibility is raised in connection with a very special sort of claim. The claim is not special in any *formal* way—the claim sentence may be quite ordinary, such as, "I know there is a tomato there." But it is special in that it explicitly is *not* made against the ordinary background of the known presence of physical things and *is* intended to function as a claim that exemplifies this background knowledge. That is, once one has conceptualized propositions (i) and (ii) of paragraph I in epistemic terms, then they will seem to express assumptions or unquestioned background beliefs, and thus it will seem that the philosopher's claim will have a different force than that possessed by our ordinary claims of the same form. Second, the possibility is necessarily considered apart from any of those factors that we would ordinarily require before seriously considering this possibility. The epistemologist feels that he must consider this possibility even though he has no reason for thinking he is actually hallucinating and does actually seriously consider this possibility completely apart from any such reason. And here I would stress that we cannot find the difference we are looking for by an examination of the situation with which the epistemologist works or of the general form of his inquiry or of the language he uses in his inquiry. For the perceptual situation is paradigmatically normal and the general form of his inquiry is the same as that of ordinary inquiries (e.g., the one previously given of claiming to know there is a robin in the oak), and his language is quite obviously just ordinary language.

Let us now return to the job of outlining the difficulties that seem to stand in the way of a direct appraisal of Dretske's ideas. It is clear, I think, that traditional epistemologists typically appeal to the hallucination possibility when examining existential claims such as "There is a tomato before me now." Dretske, however, mainly concentrates on identificatory and characterizational claims.

Thus it is not clear that if we were to agree with him that the hallucination possibility lacks some degree of relevance to *these* sorts of claims we are directly denying anything alleged by those traditional epistemologists who have insisted on raising the hallucination possibility.

In this connection we should remember that traditional epistemologists have *also* worked with identificatory and characterizational claims. But typically they have not examined *these* claims by appealing to the possibility of delusive perceptual experience. Instead they have here insisted on the possibility of future disconfirmatory observations. Their inquiries have been of the sort described as verification arguments. (That the hallucination inquiry and the verification argument are importantly different is shown not merely by the differences in claims examined and techniques of examination but also by the differences in their ultimate conclusions. The hallucination inquiry generates the sense-datum thesis about perception, whereas the verification argument shows that our empirical claims are radically predictive in nature.) Thus, if one were to answer Dretske from the general traditional position which he is opposing, one might say the following: "To attack *our* position you must either show the irrelevance of the hallucination possibility to existential empirical claims or show the irrelevance of the possibility of future disconfirmatory observation to identificatory and characterizational claims. But you seem to do neither. Rather, you only show the irrelevance of the hallucination possibility to identificatory and characterizational claims. And typically we have not appealed to that possibility in our examination of those claims."

II

I now want to turn from these general reflections to a more detailed examination of one of Dretske's claims. He says that the hallucination possibility is "simply irrelevant" to our identificatory and characterizational claims. This assertion seems to me to be slightly too strong. I think that the most he can assert is that our ability or inability to rule out the hallucination possibility is simply irrelevant to the question of whether we possess the *ability* to obtain increments in identificatory and characterizational knowledge through visual perception. But typically we do not claim that we possess this ability. Rather we claim for example that the bird is a robin or that the robin has certain wing markings. The ability we exercise in making such claims may be untouched by the hallucination possibility, but it is a further question whether our claims will always be untouched by that possibility.

Claims are made within situations and what will and will not be relevant to a claim will depend in part on the situation. Now from a commonsense point of view we must either know or have good reason to suspect that a situation has quite special features for it to be reasonable for us so much as to raise the hallucination possibility. The first question, then, is whether a claim *can* be made in a situation known or reasonably suspected to possess appropriate special features. If it can be made in such a situation then it is a claim which can be reasonably examined in the light of the hallucination possibility. I think that identificatory and characterizational claims can be made in such situations. If this is so, our next question is this: Given such a situation, will a person be required to alter or abandon his identificatory or characterizational claim if he cannot rule out the possibility of hallucination in that situation?

Now in some of these situations (taken from the ordinary point of view) the person making the claim can rule out the hallucination possibility. Consider this example: You have been working in the garden and have cut some flowers and have brought them into the house. As you were arranging them you saw that they had already become wilted. So you threw them away. Later you tell me about the flowers and say that after working with them a few minutes you saw that they were wilted and so threw them away. Also, you tell me that they were violets. I think about this. I know that no violets bloom at this time of year. I also can see that you are in a highly distraught state. And I know that you have been taking drugs which sometimes cause visual hallucinations. So I raise the possibility that you only hallucinated those violets. Here you can "rule out" this possibility in a number of ways. "Violets? No, they were lilies." "I haven't taken any drugs in the last six weeks." "Of course not—I was working with them in the garden and cut them myself and you know those drugs never cause tactile hallucinations." "Look, when you do hallucinate something with that drug it is like seeing an afterimage—you cannot look away from the thing. But I clearly remember looking away from those flowers a number of times."

In all of these ways the possibility could be ruled out. In each case the possibility is ruled out by rebutting one of the reasons in connection with which the possibility was raised. (That we ordinarily raise this possibility only in connection with some special reason and only with respect to some limited aspect of the situation is part of what makes it possible for us to "rule out" this possibility in everyday cases.)

In other situations, however, a person might not in fact be able to rule out this possibility. For example, the same person tells me that the violets on the living room table are wilted, that he had looked at them ten minutes ago and had seen that they were. I again raise the hallucination possibility with the same reasons. But this time he insists that they were violets. And this time he had not handled them and had not looked away from them and then back at them. Thus the ways mentioned above of ruling out the possibility are not available to him. Still, the situation is one in which the possibility was raised only in connection with *him*. So he brings *me* to the living room to "see for myself." But we do not find any flowers there. Of course, someone *might* have discarded them. But it is not at all certain that he did not merely hallucinate them. In this case there is a real doubt.

Now in the first case there clearly is no reason for the man to alter his claim. He was, after all, able to rule out that possibility. But can he simply maintain his claim in the second case? His claim was: "I saw that the flowers were wilted"; can he justifiably continue to make that claim?

Must he *abandon* his claim? Surely he would neither persist in his claim nor abandon it. Rather, he would adjust it. He might say: "Well, I really am not sure there were any flowers there, but if there were then they *were* wilted. If I did hallucinate flowers then I hallucinated wilted ones." That is, his claim as a whole must be adjusted, but the "is wilted" part of his claim, as Dretske points out, need not be adjusted. And there is no doubt that he has the ability to recognize wilted flowers *when* he sees them. But the claim he made cannot stand as made.

Thus it seems that if we focus on the full claim and the situation within which it is made we must say that if the hallucination possibility can be reasonably raised and cannot be ruled out then the claim must be adjusted though not simply discarded. And if this is so then it is not quite correct to say that the hallucination possibility is "simply irrelevant" to our claims, not even to our identificatory and characterizational claims.

On the other hand, it seems clear that these sorts of claims are not open to full and direct challenge by the hallucination possibility. There is a real difference between the relevance of "You might be hallucinating" to "There is a robin in the oak—I can see that one is there" and to "The robin in the oak has a broken wing—I can see that it does." If one cannot rule out the possibility in connection with the existential claim then it is not enough to adjust it—one must simply abandon it (perhaps replacing it with an expression of belief). Thus it seems that we should say neither that the hallucination possibility is simply irrelevant nor fully relevant to our commonsense identificatory and characterizational claims. Such claims can be indirectly (but only indirectly) undercut by the appeal to this possibility.

Now thus far we have spoken merely about the relevance of the hallucination possibility as *ordinarily* appealed to. What about the generalization to the philosophical appeal to that possibility? If my modification of Dretske's assertion about the irrelevance of this possibility is correct, then the generalization would take roughly this form: "Even if the hallucination inquiry of traditional epistemology were entirely valid it still would not *directly* undercut any of our commonsense perceptual claims, even those which are explicitly existential." If the epistemologist did work with genuine commonsense perceptual claims as commonly made and understood, then if his inquiry were valid it would follow that at least some of our commonsense perceptual claims can be *directly* undercut by the hallucination possibility. It therefore becomes critically essential to scrutinize the epistemologist's hallucination inquiry, for we must now either be able to show that it is not valid or that the claims with which it works are not identical in all respects with our commonsense claims.[7]

We know that epistemologists often work with existence claims

---

[7]The ordinary appeal to the hallucination possibility is only indirectly relevant to identificatory and characterizational claims. Thus one might argue that even the philosophical appeal to the hallucination possibility is only indirectly relevant to them. But the difficult cases concern those claims to which an ordinary appeal to the hallucination possibility is *directly* relevant. It is in connection with these sorts of claims that the philosophical appeal to the hallucination possibility is most tempting.

such as "There is a tomato here." Formally, these claims would seem to fall within the class of such ordinary claims as "There is a robin in the oak," "There is a stick over there," etc. Dretske gives an example of such a claim, namely, "There is a bug in the soup." Further, epistemologists will initially give their claims a perceptual basis such as "I know there is a tomato there because I can see it." We here meet that so-called nonpropositional use of "see" that Dretske said he would not discuss. I find it odd that he does not consider this use (if it is that) of "see" for, first, it is the use that is central to the traditional hallucination inquiry ("What kinds of things do we really see?") and, second, it is a very common use in connection with ordinary claims. In many cases if we ask someone how he knows there is a robin in the oak or a tomato on the table or a bug in his soup or a log blocking the road he would answer by saying, "I can see one there." It is not, after all, just philosophers who formulate their perceptual reports with sentences involving the nonpropositional use of "see." I believe that one of the main reasons he would give for concentrating on the "see that" construction is that the truth of "He sees that ∅" implies that he knows that ∅. But a discussion of this would lead away from the point at hand and Dretske himself works with "I can see that there is a bug in the soup" and this, at least, does not seem to differ materially from "I see that there is a bug in the soup."

At this stage, therefore, it seems fairly clear that the sentences used by the epistemologist in setting forth his claim and basis are the same as the sentences we commonly use in setting forth some of our claims and bases. For example: My wife is about to go shopping and she asks me if there are any tomatoes left. I reply, in a quite absent-minded tone of voice, that there are. Knowing me pretty well she asks me if I am quite sure there are. I reply, "Yes, yes, I know there are some left—I can see them over there on the table." So if we are to differentiate between the claim that the epistemologist makes and those that we ordinarily make we must look beyond the sentences we employ and their formal features.

Further, the perceptual situation within which we might make some perfectly commonsensical perceptual claim may be identical with the perceptual situation considered by the epistemologist. The perceptual situation will be one of a man standing before some public item with his eyes open and focused in the direction of the item and with nothing blocking his view, etc.[8] That is, the philosopher will work with a paradigmatically normal perceptual situation of the type within which we often make commonsense perceptual claims. Thus the philosopher's claim not only cannot be differentiated in terms of the sentence he employs, it also cannot be differentiated by an appeal to the perceptual situation within which he employs it.

So what is the difference between the epistemologist's claim "I know there is a tomato there" and the commonsense claim "I know there is a tomato there"? We may easily enough be able to *sense* some difference, but it seems very difficult to *describe* the difference with precision and in detail and in such a way as not to prejudice either our view of the philosopher's claim or of the commonsense claim.

Now we might want to say that the claims really are identical. If we say this and agree that the philosopher's appeal to the hallucination possibility (e.g., within the framework of the hallucination inquiry described above) does radically undercut *his* claim (e.g., as made at the beginning of that inquiry), then we would have to agree that many of our ordinary claims are radically undercut by this possibility whether or not we acknowledge this in everyday life. So if we say that the claims are identical and still want to argue that our commonsense claims cannot be directly undercut by appeal to the hallucination possibility, we will have to show that there is something wrong with the philosophical appeal to the hallucination possibility. But to show this we would have to make some distinction between ordinary and philosophical appeals to this possibility, and Dretske does not draw this distinction. Thus it would seem that we must try instead to discover some difference between the philosophical "I know there is a tomato here because I can see one here" and the commonsensical "I know there is a tomato here because I can see that one is here."

[8] The most natural way of indicating a normal perceptual situation is to use the form of words "Here so-and-so sees the tomato." But to say this is to beg the question of the perceptual status of the things around us. Thus I have tried to indicate indirectly the sort of situation I have in mind by saying, "Nothing is blocking his view," etc. One might take my "description" as simply a couple of remarks intended to remind you of these very standard situations. I certainly do not mean to imply that one might be able to pinpoint a normal perceptual situation by ruling out *every* abnormal feature. There is no "every" here.

In this way we will follow up on Dretske's aim of becoming "quite clear as to what is and what is not being claimed in our ordinary perceptual reports" by seeing how what they claim is not exactly what the epistemologist would claim.

As mentioned above, the philosopher views his claim sentence as expressing a commonsense belief. By this, however, he does not mean that his sentence expresses exactly the sort of claim it would be used to express in ordinary circumstances. His claim is not one of Dretske's "commonsense claims." When the philosopher says, "I know there is a tomato here," he is presenting his knowledge that a tomato is present as an *example* of the sort of thing we believe we know. On the other hand, the ordinary claim that a tomato is present does not function as an example of anything. This difference in part comes out in our feeling that if the philosopher's claim is undercut by the hallucination possibility then there is reason for *general* doubt. But we do not feel that when some particular, ordinary claim is undercut by the hallucination possibility there is then reason for doubting anything beyond that particular claim.

I think Dretske's remarks reflect this sort of difference in a number of ways. He speaks, for example, of how, in our use of demonstratives, we convey the information that what we point out is "something that you and other people can also see." (This is clearly connected with proposition (ii) about our perception of *public* items.) He also says that the responsibility for our "starting points" rests with our entire information-gathering resources. Our "starting points" are not, in general, questioned, and when in particular circumstances and for special reasons some "starting point" is questioned the questioning does not spread to all "starting points." If I say, "The flowers were wilted," I take as my "starting point" that some flowers were there. Now this might be questioned. But in questioning this (e.g., via the hallucination possibility) it is not questioned that the table is there or that I am speaking with you. Thus other "starting points" are always available; for example, we can go to the *table,* you can ask whether *I* saw some flowers there, etc. (The "starting points" really form a kind of background matrix of public, physical items *against* which we make our particular claims. This is connected with proposition (i) about the existence of public, physical items.)

In these and various other ways Dretske seems to suggest that there is a certain level or dimension of information or common knowledge in terms of which we make our commonsense perceptual claims but which itself never becomes the object of explicit commonsense claims. Our commonsense claim that there is a robin in the oak or a tomato on the table will be made against this sort of background, and thus the *perceptual* claim "I can see one there" or "I can see that one is there" will be entirely satisfactory given (a) that we know robins or tomatoes when we see them and (b) that there is no special reason for thinking that in this case we have suffered a delusion of sight. (That is, our perceptual claim will stand, given that there is no reason for thinking that what is generally true about sight—that it picks up public objects— does not hold in this case.[9])

In contrast, epistemologists seem to try to crystallize this background into a particular claim and thus produce a claim which cannot, as it were, rely on this background. The philosopher represents the whole background with a particular claim (of a quite ordinary form) and thus *his* claim simply is not made against the background. His claim therefore will seem to "probe foundations" in a way that no ordinary claim will and his claim will carry a weight never carried by any ordinary claim.

Undoubtedly Dretske would reject or at least seriously question this sort of philosophical view. But I think he might agree that what the philosopher tries to claim is far beyond what we ever ordinarily claim. His disagreement with the epistemologist, then, might be of one of these two kinds: (a) He might argue that this background information or common knowledge *cannot* be expressed through a claim (in which case the epistemologist either fails to make any claim or misunderstands the claim he does make), or (b) he might argue that this background information can be established through our total information-gathering resources in such a way that the hallucination possibility raises no particular difficulty.

---

[9]One might put this in terms of a legal metaphor. It is fundamental to our legal system that a man is innocent until proven guilty and that he is not required to defend his innocence until evidence of guilt is presented. Analogously, a man's perception is of a public object until it is proven that he has suffered a perceptual delusion and he need not defend his claim to see a public object until evidence that he has suffered a delusion is presented. The prima facie background to the law is that a man is innocent. The prima facie background to common empirical knowledge is (in part) that we perceive public objects. This, of course, is *only* a metaphor.

Indeed, these two ideas are not exclusive of one another. It might be argued that we must both explore and show the solidity of the foundations of our common knowledge and then criticize traditional epistemology in terms of its attempt to do this in a far too narrowing way (e.g., by exploring the foundations through particular claim assessments). I think that there are elements of both of these ideas in Dretske's paper.

As mentioned earlier, Dretske speaks of the information conveyed in our use of demonstratives. He clearly is thinking of simple perceptual situations and the information he mentions is that the "that" which the speaker sees and to which he refers is something others can also see, i.e., it is a public item. This, of course, runs directly counter to the perceptual conclusion of the hallucination inquiry, i.e., the conclusion that the items an individual sees are private sense-datum items. And as was also mentioned earlier, he concentrates attention on the "see that" locution, a locution of recognition. Thus it is suggested that at least some of our basic "starting points" are established through sight and that sight determines some item of discourse as a public item. We might think of "I see that there is a bug in the soup" as having the force of "I see *that* and it is a bug and is in the soup" and that *it* is a bug is given by "I see that it is a bug." In this way, seeing that there is a bug in the soup will be a matter of sight locating a public item for the "starting point" of some segment of discourse and "seeing that" functioning to identify that public item as a bug. And on this view *that* some public item is present is *not* part of what is explicitly *claimed*. Yet the traditional epistemologist would seem to want to make this the basic point of his claim. Of course it is not true that we *never,* in everyday life, explicitly claim that some public item is present. We can be forced to make this—which normally is implicit—explicit in *special* cases. These would be cases in which there is some reason for thinking we may be suffering a delusion of sight. And to defend the explicit claim that a public item is present the person would then have to rule out the possibility that he is suffering some delusion of sight. But he need not do that in general. The question will be, for example, about the alleged bug but not about the soup and the bowl and the napkins and his fellows at the table, etc. In these sorts of ways Dretske seems to suggest that none of our commonsense perceptual claims, even the most explicitly existential ones, claims exactly what the philosopher would want to claim.

On the other hand Dretske also speaks of our total information-gathering resources and seems to suggest that if we properly understand the relations and functions of all of the senses and of memory and intelligence and inference, etc., then we shall see that the background of common knowledge against which we typically operate is entirely secure and either has been or can be put on a philosophically firm footing.

Perhaps the main difficulty with both of these lines of thought is due entirely to the fact that Dretske was working under severe limitations of space. Yet the fact is that both lines of thought are barely sketched. The latter line of thought is particularly vague and as presented seems entirely open to a phenomenalist interpretation. And by a "phenomenalist interpretation" I would mean an interpretation that would examine the full range of our information-gathering resources in connection with such "perceptual theses" as that we perceive only sense data, have memory experiences logically independent of the events alleged to be remembered, etc. The former line of thought, on the other hand, seems to require not only the sort of detailed examination of our commonsense claims given by Dretske but also a thoroughgoing comparison with the claims and investigations of traditional epistemology. And this would require step by step comparisons of the *claims* examined by philosophers and the claims we commonly make; of the perceptual situations common to both philosophical and commonsense claims; of the contexts in which claims are made in and out of philosophy; of the different ways in which the hallucination possibility functions in philosophical and commonsense examinations of claims, etc. For it seems to me likely that, short of knowing *exactly* and in *detail* what is going on when a philosopher submits our common knowledge to sceptical examination, no amount of careful scrutiny of ordinary claims could hope to show that the philosopher's sceptical considerations are "simply irrelevant." And, more important, nothing short of this sort of examination could hope to prove that the ultimate sense-datum thesis of the hallucination inquiry is incorrect.

Reply

FRED I. DRETSKE

Here is a muddled argument that some people find persuasive: Suppose *S*, in telling us how he knows that the piece of fruit on the table is a tomato, avows that he can see that it is a tomato. Now, as we all know, a tomato is the sort of thing which other people can see, touch, and eat; it is juicy and has a distinctive taste. It is, indeed, quite a different thing from an hallucinatory tomato or a wax imitation. Clearly, then, if *S* does *know* that it (what he sees) is a tomato, he must know that it is not merely a wax imitation, not merely a figment of his own imagination. And if he knows this in virtue of *seeing* that it is so (as he says), then he must be able to see that it is *not* an imitation, *not* merely some visual delusion. Surely, however, he cannot do this. In a spirit of generosity we might concede that he knows it is a tomato (perhaps he poked his finger in it, smelled it, tasted it, and so on), but he cannot do what he said he did—*see that it is a tomato.* This implies he can do something that he cannot do: differentiate, *on visual grounds alone,* between real tomatoes and their hallucinatory counterparts, between real tomatoes and wax reproductions. He cannot do this because, as we all know, hallucinatory tomatoes and imitation tomatoes are just the sort of thing that may be *visually indistinguishable* from real tomatoes. How can *S* see that something is a tomato when tomatoes are *visually* indistinguishable from a variety of nontomatoes?

There is a pattern to this argument and it goes something like this. If *S* knows that *x* is a foozit, and he knows this because (as he says) he can see that it is a foozit, then he must be able to see that it is not a nonfoozit. If, however, there are nonfoozits which look exactly like the foozits, then *S* cannot (despite what he says) see that anything is a foozit. He might *know* it is a foozit (by handling it, consulting experts, etc.), but he cannot see that it is, for there are nonfoozits which are visually indistinguishable from the foozits. If gin and vodka look the same to me, then I cannot see whether the liquid is gin or vodka (although I may discover which is the vodka by *tasting* or by *listening* to the testimony of a reliable informant). Likewise, if hallucinatory tomatoes and imitation tomatoes are the sorts of thing which are *visually* indistinguishable from real tomatoes, then one cannot see that something is a real tomato. There is nothing visually *distinctive* about real tomatoes, nothing that would allow S to identify a real tomato on purely visual grounds as the claim "I can see that it is a tomato" would suggest.

It is this type of argument to which my paper was addressed. The fallacy it embodies is of the kind I described. It mistakenly supposes that if something's being a P entails that it is also Q, then if S sees that something is P (and, hence, *knows* that it is P), he must also be able to see that it is Q. The above argument exploits this fallacious line of reasoning by arguing that if something's being a tomato entails that it is not an imitation, not some piece of mental imagery, then if S sees that something is a tomato, he must also see that it is not an imitation, not a figment of his own imagination. This is a mistaken inference. When S sees that *the piece of fruit* is a tomato, there is nothing in his achievement as so described which implies that S ruled out, or was even *capable* of ruling out, such alternatives *on visual grounds,* nothing to suggest that he could see that it was a real tomato in contrast to an hallucinatory one, nothing to suggest that there is anything *visually* distinctive about real tomatoes as compared to wax reproductions. The only demand such an achievement (as so described) imposes on S's visual capacities is that he be able to distinguish, on visual grounds alone, between pieces of fruit which are tomatoes and *pieces of fruit* which are not tomatoes. And to the question of whether or not he possesses *this* capacity, the subject of hallucinations and clever imitations is simply irrelevant; for wax imitations and hallucinatory figments are not, I take it, to be numbered among the pieces of fruit in this world.

It may be helpful to look at the point in this way. Let "p" be the statement "The water in the pot is boiling" and "q" the statement "The liquid in the pot is boiling water." Suppose we agree that "p" and "q" are logically equivalent. Now, S may succeed in seeing that *p*, but he may be totally *unable* to see that *q*. Why is this so? Because although "*p*" and "*q*" are logically equivalent, they represent *different increments* of information when embedded in the context "*S* sees that. . . ." And since the locution "*S* sees that . . ." (when used to tell us how *S* knows that . . .) tells us *how S* acquired this increment of information (i.e., visually), a shift in the "magnitude" of this increment is of crucial significance in understanding what *S* has done—even though the *resultant* piece of knowledge ("*p*" and "*q*") is the same (logically) in either case. What I tried to argue in my paper was that certain traditional considerations involving hallucinations, fakes, imitations, mirages, reflections, etc. are frequently, though not always, irrelevant to whether a human being can acquire these increments of information *by purely visual means*. And if these considerations are irrelevant to this matter, they are therefore irrelevant to what we can see to be the case (and, hence, *know* to be the case) since our descriptions of what we see to be the case are descriptions of *how* we have bridged these increments.

Hugly takes me to task for not distinguishing between the ordinary appeal to the "hallucination possibility" and the philosophical appeal. In one respect I think this criticism is a bit unfair; in another respect it is entirely warranted. I think it unfair because it never occurred to me that I might be interpreted as denying the (occasional) relevance of ordinary appeals to the hallucination possibility. I certainly did not wish to suggest that people never suffer hallucinations, nor that when they do they sometimes think they see things (to be the case) which are not the case. When my intoxicated companion "sees" orange bugs all over the carpet, we obviously cannot dismiss the possibility of hallucination. At least I never entertained such a thought. I only wished to consider the plausibility of a view that takes its cue from such situations and draws conclusions, general conclusions, about the epistemic credentials of ordinary perceptual claims. And the kind of conclusion which has been drawn from a consideration of such cases is that the visual experience which provides the basis for epistemic perceptual claims is conspicuously inadequate to support the implied claims to knowledge. The conclusion is drawn that even when we are *not* hallucinating, even when *it is* (or may be) a tomato which we see, the associated visual experience is not *itself* (see my opening argument) an adequate epistemic basis for saying we *know* that it is a tomato. And since the claim to see that *x* is a tomato implies that the claimant has discovered *x* to be a tomato in some distinctively visual fashion, a simple application of *modus tollens* generates the conclusion that we do not (ever) really see that something is a tomato.

There is a variety of ways of dealing with this sceptical argument, one of the most fashionable being to insist that we common folk have our own epistemological standards for knowing, and anything that satisfies these standards qualifies as knowledge. We know (for all practical purposes, and these are the only purposes that are relevant) that it is a tomato when we see it (sometimes), and never mind about the carping of the epistemologists. Without judging the value of this approach, I have tried to urge an examination of some *preliminary* matters; namely, that if we look at what we common folk say we see (to be the case), instead of concentrating on what such claims imply we know, we will find that what we describe ourselves as doing is only acquiring a modest portion (increment) of that information which the claim itself implies that we possess. What we describe ourselves as having *discovered* by *visual* means is (generally speaking) only a small piece of that information which our claim itself implies that we have. In a word, what we claim to have done is something which the possibility of visual hallucinations, and very often the possibility of fakes, forgeries, imitations, and reflections, has not the slightest tendency to show cannot be done in a purely visual fashion with the *highest* epistemic credentials.

There is another respect, however, in which Hugly's queries are justified. We often say, "I could see that . . ." or "I can see that . . .," meaning by this (as far as I can tell) nothing different (when this is understood to be a description of how we know that . . .) from "I saw that . . ." or "I see that. . . ." In my paper I moved freely back and forth between both modes of expression. Ordinarily this might not have been objectionable, but, with respect to the point I was after, an important ambiguity appears. I wished to argue that the possibility of hallucinatory tomatoes or imitation tomatoes was irrelevant to whether *S could see* that a piece of fruit was a tomato in the sense of "could" which might be rendered as "has the ability to." Is the *possibility* (let us even say the *probability*) of hallucinations or fake tomatoes (visually indistinguishable from real tomatoes) relevant to whether S has the capacity to *know* that a piece of fruit is a tomato by seeing that it is a tomato? Is it relevant to whether S can bridge the increment which such a statement depicts him as bridging? Hugly correctly points out that my argument only shows that various sceptical considerations are irrelevant to whether we possess this *ability*. And this, of course, is what I intended to show. For in doing this I hoped to show that there was nothing in such considerations which tended to show that there was some fundamental epistemological inadequacy in those situations where we describe ourselves as knowing something to be the case by seeing it to be the case. I admit, though, that my indiscriminate use of "could" and "can" helped to obscure this point.

Hugly also wonders why I do not consider the so-called nonpropositional use of the verb "to see." He finds this odd because, as he says, it is the use which is central to the traditional hallucination inquiry. I do not care for the terminology "propositional" and "nonpropositional,"[1] but since I introduced it let me persevere and indicate why I avoided talking about nonpropositional seeing. Suppose S sees a robin in the oak. Does he know there is a robin in the oak? Notice, this question is perfectly sensible. Obviously S does not have to identify *everything* he sees. He also saw fourteen robins, two bluejays, and a crow flying over the cornfield. Does he know what kinds of birds they were or how many? No. They flew by so quickly, and they were a hundred yards away. Of course, if S says, "I saw a robin in the oak today," there is a strong presumption that he *saw that* it was a robin—especially if he says this in response to a question such as "How do you know there were any birds in the oak?" But this is little more than a *presumption*. A similar presumption operates when he says, "I touched (ate, shot, stepped on, etc.) a robin today." There is nothing about such statements that is of particular epistemological significance. One can touch (eat, shoot, or step on) a robin without knowing it is a robin, but our *saying* such things is significant since it implies (in some sense) that we have identified the item in question as a robin. To use another of Hugly's examples, if my wife calls to me from the other room and wants to know

[1] Is seeing the trouble, a difference, the problem, the answer, or what is on the table a "propositional" or "nonpropositional" use of the verb "to see"?

whether I am certain that there are any tomatoes left, I can reply in a variety of ways: "Yes, Jim and I are playing catch with them," "Yes, I just sat on them," and so on. Does the fact that such utterances function perfectly well as responses to the question "Are you sure (how do you know) there are any tomatoes left?" show that "playing catch with *x*" or "sitting on *x*" represent important epistemic relations that we bear to objects? Of course not. It merely means that, given a reasonably alert adult, such "involvements" with *x* are sufficiently intimate to justify the assumption that the person involved knows what *x* is, and this is especially so if *x* is some familiar object like a tomato. Likewise, when the average adult sees a tomato (under more or less normal conditions, close at hand) he is likely to see *what* it is—see that it is a tomato.

The nonpropositional use of the verb "to see" is, in an important respect, *epistemically neutral*. We can see an *X* without realizing that it is an *X*. We can also *truly* say, "I see (saw) an *X*," *without* knowing (without even believing) that it is (was) an *X* we see (saw). Consider the pickpocket at the bus stop who says, "I see the bus coming," in order to distract the attention of the people standing with him. He can truly say this (that distant vehicle he sees *is* the bus) without believing it. Seeing an *X* is like being on the pier when the boat arrives; although both states of affairs are epistemically neutral, we can answer the question "How do you know there was an *X* there?" by saying, "I saw an *X* there," and we can answer the question "How do you know the boat arrived?" by saying, "I was there on the pier when it arrived."

This brings me to the most important point about the nonpropositional use of this verb. Hugly is right when he says that it has played a major role in hallucination inquiries. But this is just the trouble. By conflating "seeing an *X*" with "seeing that it is an *X*" one is mistakenly led to suppose that epistemological considerations are relevant to whether we see tomatoes, bugs (in our soup), robins (in the oak), and so on. That is, one will suppose that if there are sceptical arguments which tend to show that we cannot know for certain that what we are seeing is a robin in the oak, if we cannot *see that* there is a robin in the oak, then those same arguments tend to show that we do not see *a robin* in the oak. This ridiculous argument (preparatory to the introduction of sense data) can only get off the ground if we confuse seeing a robin in the oak with seeing that there is a robin in the oak, if we confuse seeing a tomato with seeing that it is a tomato. *Nothing* I had to say in my paper was relevant to whether we see tomatoes, bugs, robins, water, or people. Whether people *do* see such things is as much an epistemological issue as, and no more than, whether people step on bugs, feed robins, drink water, or stand next to people.

We cannot show that *S* does not see a robin in the oak because he does not know, or does not believe, that there is a robin in the oak. (Think of *S* as a small child.) We could as well show that *S* is not standing next to an oak tree because he does not know, does not believe, it is an oak tree. The most that we could show by this is that *S* has no basis for *saying* he sees a robin. But this is true of almost any claim *S* might advance, and it shows nothing distinctive about what it means to *see* something. The same could be said about his statement "I stepped on an ant today." It is for the purpose of avoiding this confusion that I concentrated on those perceptual claims which do tell us, explicitly, that the percipient *discovered* something about what he saw, and discovered it in a distinctively visual manner.

There is, finally, the question of existential claims. Hugly is correct in pointing out that I concentrated heavily on what he calls "identificatory" and "characterizational" claims. My excuse is that my point was easier to illustrate in these cases. But I do not think my thesis, the notion that epistemic perceptual claims are always incremental in character, is restricted to identificatory and characterizational nominals, and I tried to indicate this briefly with the example of a bug in the soup. Existential objects of the verb "to see" generally take the form of seeing that there is a so-and-so *in, on, next to, near, talking to, under, following, watching, touching,* . . . such-and-such. I saw that there was someone *talking to* the widow, that there was a robin in the oak, that there was a dog *following* the man, that there was some money on the table. What I tried to indicate, perhaps with excessive brevity, is that, once again, there is a particular increment embodied in each of these objects of the verb. When *S* says that he can see that there is a robin in the oak, he has certainly told us *how* he knows that there is a robin in the oak. But has he told us *how* he knows that it is an oak that the robin is in? Must he be able to *see that* the tree is an oak to see that there is a robin in the oak? No. Presumably, he knows it is an oak—after all, he did refer to it as an oak—but he *may* have learned that it was an oak (or that it was a tree, or even that it was a *real* tree) in a variety of non-visual ways. His friend may have *told* him it was an oak. Must one be able to see that a woman is a widow to see that there is someone talking to the widow? Must I be able to see that it is *your* bird house (or *a* bird house) to see that there is a robin in (on, near) your bird house? What these rhetorical questions are designed to reveal is that existential objects of the verb also embody an increment of information, an increment which the entire statement describes the percipient as acquiring in a distinctively visual manner. When *S* tells us that he sees that there is a robin in the oak, *S* does *not* tell us *how* he knows that he is seeing an oak (a tree, or even a *real* tree). And since he has not told us this, he has not told us *how he knows* what his perceptual statement implies that he knows: that he is not hallucinating the *entire affair* (robin *and* oak tree). In a sense, he has told us how he went from one piece of information, "That is an oak tree," to another piece of information, "There is a robin in the oak."[2] There is nothing in *S*'s achievement as so described which implies that *S* was able to visually differentiate between a real robin in a real oak tree and an hallucinatory robin in an hallucinatory oak tree, nothing to suggest that he was able to eliminate the possibility of some *comprehensive* visual delusion in any distinctively *visual* way (although his perceptual statement implies that he knows that he is not suffering from comprehensive visual delusion). In order to see that there is a robin in the oak *S* must only

[2]In some cases, of course, *S* may not have learned it was an oak until later; *at the time* he saw the robin in it he did not know it was an oak. In such cases the actual increment which *S* bridged in seeing that there was a robin in the oak may be different from that reflected by the actual terms which appear in the factive nominal. What term or phrase we select to refer to what we see to be *P* (in this case: what we see to have a robin in it) is affected by several variables, one of the most important being the ease with which our listeners will be able to identify what it is that was seen to be *P*. There are complexities here which I do not have the space to discuss. I tried to indicate the location of some of these difficulties in the last paragraph of my paper when I mentioned the complications that arise when we turn to reports in the past tense and in the third person. I do not believe, however, that these complexities affect (adversely) the point I am trying to make.

be able to discover, on visual grounds alone, whether *this oak tree* has a robin in it. And, to the question of whether or not he possesses *this* capacity, the possibility of some comprehensive visual delusion (i.e., the *whole* scene—robin *and* oak tree) is simply irrelevant.

This brings me to the point of my distinction between "seeing that there is a bug in my soup" and "seeing that it is a bug that is in my soup." Notice the very real difference between these two achievements. Unlike the explicit existential, the latter does not (even) tell us *how* the percipient knows that there is something in his soup; it only tells us how he discovered that *the something in his soup* was a bug rather than anything else. To take a concrete case, suppose everyone agrees that there is something in your bird house; the question remains "What?" I see nothing overly ambitious in *S*, a fellow given over to hallucinations and currently under the influence of drugs, seeing that it is a robin that is in the bird house. This achievement demands nothing more from *S* than the ability to distinguish, on visual grounds, between robins, bluejays, wrens, squirrels, etc.—between the sorts of things which *might* be *in* the bird house. Hence, *S*'s tendency to hallucinate birds, snakes, and other strange creatures in the middle of normal surroundings (eidetic imagery) does not in the least detract from his ability to see that it is a robin that is in your bird house. For, of course, hallucinatory creatures are not *in* real bird houses. Hence, *S* may be quite able to see that *it is a robin* that is in your bird house without being able to see that *there is a robin* in your bird house, for the latter achievement demands something more from *S*, it represents a larger increment. To see that *there is a robin* in the bird house one must not only be able to see that it is a robin that is in the bird house, one must also be able to see that there is, indeed, something in the bird house. A person given over to eidetic imagery may not be able to arrive at this latter piece of information on purely visual grounds. The point could be put this way: when *S* sees that it is a robin that is in the bird house, he knows that there is a robin in the bird house; nevertheless, he may not (because of various afflictions) be able to see that there is a robin in the bird house. Once again we have a case in which "*p*" and "*q*" are equivalent but, by virtue of representing different increments, *S* is able to see that *p* but is not able to see that *q*.

I should stress once again that I have not argued for the claim that *S can* acquire the increments his perceptual reports imply that he has acquired in a distinctively visual manner. It is a further question whether philosophical scepticism can get a foothold in this area, whether *S* can go from the fact that this is water to the fact that this water is boiling (the increment involved in his seeing that the water is boiling) by purely *visual* means, whether he can *visually* bridge the gap between the fact that this is a piece of fruit and the fact that this piece of fruit is a tomato (the increment involved in seeing that the piece of fruit is a tomato), whether he can tell on visual grounds alone whether an oak tree (a real oak tree) has a robin in it. All I hope to have done is to have called attention to the fact that such increments exist, and that what we describe ourselves as doing when we describe what we have seen to be the case is acquiring *such increments* of information in a distinctively visual way.

If I may close with a slight extension of the analogy I suggested in the opening paragraph of my paper, it seems to me that the philosophic sceptic is sometimes in the position of a man who is puzzled by the presence on Times Square of an African chief. What puzzles him is the fact that the fellow said he got there *by walking*. Now the sceptic has a proof to show that this is impossible; there is, as he well knows, a large body of water separating Africa and Times Square, and no man can walk on water. The trouble here is that our sceptic never thought to ask where our African chief *walked from*.[3] If he walked *from* 32nd

---

[3]One of the easiest (and most used) devices for obscuring this crucial piece of information in perceptual statements is the practice of conflating the "propositional" and the "nonpropositional" use of the verb "to see." That is, instead of working with the statement "*S* sees that the water is boiling," one transforms this into "*S* sees the boiling water" with the understanding that this latter is supposed to describe an epistemic achievement on *S*'s part. We are now in the position of being told that *S* knows that it (what he sees) is boiling water, but we are not told (as we are in the former report) where he came *from* in arriving at this knowledge. Did he see that the water was boiling (and, hence, know that it was boiling water)? Did he see that the liquid was boiling water (and, hence, know that it was boiling water)? Did he, perhaps, see that the boiling liquid was water (and, hence, know that it was boiling water)? To attempt to describe all of these *different* achievements with the locution "*S* sees the boiling water" is to suppress the crucial incremental character of what he has done.

Street and Broadway, of course, our sceptic's proofs about the impossibility of the man's doing what he said he did are going to be totally irrelevant. What I tried to suggest in my paper was that some of the traditional sceptical objections to our seeing (to be the case) what we think and say we see (to be the case) are irrelevant for the same reasons.

The Loose and Popular and the Strict and Philosophical Senses of Identity

RODERICK M. CHISHOLM

I

I take the expressions used in the title of this paper from Bishop Butler's Dissertation entitled "Of Personal Identity."[1] According to Butler, it will be recalled, when we say of a physical thing existing at one time that it is identical with, or the same as, a physical thing existing at some other time ("This is the same ship that we traveled on before."), we are using the expression "the same as" or "identical with" in a "loose and popular sense." But when we say of a person existing at one time that he is identical with, or the same as, a person existing at some other time ("The ship still has the same captain it had before."), we are using "the same as" or "identical with" in a "strict and philosophical sense." I believe there is an element of truth in both theses and shall discuss them in turn.

II

To illustrate Butler's first thesis, that it is only in a loose and popular sense that we may speak of the identity of a physical thing through time, let us update the traditional problem of the ship of Theseus. We start with a ship made entirely of wood and give it the name "The U.S.S. South Dakota." Then one day a

[1]Dissertation I, in *The Whole Works of Joseph Butler, LL.D* (London, 1839), pp. 263–70. But compare Locke's third letter to the Bishop of Worcester: "For it being his body both before and after the resurrection, everyone ordinarily speaks of his body as the same, though, in a strict and philosophical sense, as your lordship speaks, it be not the very same."

wooden plank is cast off and replaced by an aluminum one. Since the change is only slight, there is no question as to the survival of the U.S.S. South Dakota. We still have the ship we had before; the ship that we have now is the same as the ship that we had before. On another day, another wooden plank is cast off and also replaced by an aluminum one. Still the same ship, since, as before, the change is only slight. The changes continue, in a similar way, and finally the U.S.S. South Dakota is made entirely of aluminum. The aluminum ship, one may well argue, *is* the wooden ship we started with, for the ship we started with survived each particular change, and identity, after all, is transitive.

But what happened to the discarded wooden planks? Consider this possibility, which Thomas Hobbes suggested: "If some man had kept the old planks as they were taken out, and by putting them afterwards together in the same order, had again made a ship of them, this, without doubt, had also been the same numerical ship with that which was at the beginning; and so there would have been two ships numerically the same, which is absurd."[2] Assuming, as perhaps one has no right to do, that each of the wooden planks survived intact throughout these changes, one might well argue that the reassembled wooden ship *is* the ship that we started with. "After all, it is made up of the very same parts, standing in the very same relations, whereas that ugly aluminum object doesn't have a single part in common with our original ship."

To compound the problem still further, let us suppose that the captain of the original ship had solemnly taken the vow that, if his ship were ever to go down, he would go down with it. What, now, if the two ships collide at sea and he sees them start to sink together? Where does his duty lie—with the aluminum ship or with the reassembled wooden ship?

"The carriage" is another ancient version of the problem. Socrates and Plato change the parts of their carriages piece by piece until, finally, Socrates' carriage is made up of all the parts of Plato's original carriage and Plato's carriage is made up of all the parts of Socrates' original carriage. Have they exchanged their carriages or not, and if so, at what point? Also, there is the castle William Randolph Hearst had disassembled, with each

[2]Thomas Hobbes, *Concerning Body*, chap. XI ("Of Identity and Difference"), sec. 7.

stone carefully labeled and identified, then shipped off to San Simeon, California, and displayed there as being the very same castle as one that once stood in a certain historical spot in Europe. Can we now say that there is a building in California more than 700 years old? And there is the reconstructed Santa Trinita bridge in Florence, which was built, in part at least, from stones preserved from the bridge that had been there for 400 years.[3] Can one still say that the Santa Trinita bridge is more than 400 years old? Or, again, which of the two restaurants in Philadelphia is really the original Bookbinder's? And, finally, there is the child playing with his blocks. He builds a house with ten blocks, uses it as a garrison for his toy soldiers, disassembles it, builds many other things, then builds a house again, with each of the ten blocks occupying the position it had occupied before, and he uses it again as a garrison for his soldiers. Was the house that was destroyed the same as the one that subsequently came into being?

These puzzles which concern the persistence of objects through periods of time have their analogues for the extension of objects through places in space. Consider the river that is known in New Orleans as "the Mississippi." Most of us would say that the source of the river is in northern Minnesota. But what if one were to argue instead that the source is in Montana, where it is known as "the Missouri"? Or that its source is in Pittsburgh, where it is known as "the Ohio," or that its source is farther back where it is called "the Allegheny," or in still another place, where it is called "the Monongahela."?[4]

The accompanying diagram provides us with a schematic illustration.

```
    (a)     (b)     (c)
     x       x       x
          x  x  x
          x x x
             x
             x
             x
            (d)
```

[3] I take this example from Sydney Shoemaker, *Self-Knowledge and Self-Identity* (Ithaca, N.Y., 1963), p. 28.
[4] Cf. W. V. Quine: "Thus take the question of the biggest fresh lake. Is Michigan-Huron admissible, or is it a pair of lakes? . . . Then take the

Of the river that has its southern point at (*d*), one might wonder whether it flows southeasterly from (*a*), or due south from (*b*), or southwesterly from (*c*). (For simplicity, we ignore the Allegheny and the Monongahela.) If we are puzzled about the beginning of the Mississippi, we should be equally puzzled about the end of the Rhine. Now, reading our diagram from bottom to top (and again oversimplifying), we may say that if the Rhine begins at (*d*), then it ends either with the Maas at (*a*), or with the Waal at (*b*), or with the Lek at (*c*).[5]

Perhaps we can imagine three philosophers looking down at the river(s) that end(s) at (*d*). One insists that the river flows between (*a*) and (*d*), another that it flows between (*b*) and (*d*), and the third that it flows between (*c*) and (*d*); and each insists that, since the arms (or tributaries) to which the other two philosophers refer are distinct not only from each other but from the river itself, neither of the other two can be right. Their dispute, clearly, would be analogous in significant respects to the problem of the ship of Theseus.

What are we to say of such puzzles? We might follow the extreme course that Carneades took and simply deny the principle of the transitivity of identity.[6] But let us proceed more slowly. We may begin by considering certain general principles about compound things—things that are made up of other things.

III

Unfortunately, most recent discussions of these matters are based upon what seems to me to be an excessively liberal ontology. It is assumed that there are those strange wholes that Brentano

---

question of the longest river. Is the Mississippi-Missouri admissible, or is it a river and a half?" (*Word and Object* [New York, 1960], p. 128).

[5]Using terms not commonly applied to rivers, we may note for future reference that when our diagram is read from top to bottom it illustrates *fusion* and when it is read from bottom to top it illustrates *fission*.

[6]See Note C of the article "Carneades" in Pierre Bayle's *A General Dictionary: Historical and Critical,* trans. Rev. J. P. Bernard, Rev. Thomas Birch, John Lockeman, *et al.* (10 vols.; London, 1734–41): "He found uncertainty in the most evident notions. All logicians know that the foundation of the syllogism, and consequently the faculty of reasoning, is built on this maxim: Those things which are identical with a third are the same with each other (*Quae sunt idem uno tertio sunt idem inter se*). It is certain that Carneades opposed it strongly and displayed all his subtleties against it."

called "collectiva," also sometimes "conjuctiva." If a philosopher thinks that there are conjunctiva, or collectiva, he will say that, for any two individual things, A and B, there is that conjunctivum consisting of just A and B, and that this, too, is an individual thing.[7] Thus if A is a man in South Dakota and B is a horse in northern Ireland, then there is that conjunctivum, A and B, made up of just the man and the horse. This conjunctivum is not to be thought of as an abstract object; it is not the class whose sole members are the man and the horse. It is concrete in just the sense in which the man is concrete and the horse is concrete. If the man weighs 200 pounds and the horse 2,000, then the conjunctivum weighs 2,200. And the man and the horse will itself be a part of ever so many other conjunctiva—for example, the conjunctivum that is made up of the man and the horse and a certain stick or stone. Thus McTaggart assumed that among the things in the world there is that "substance" which "consists of a table now in Cambridge, a rabbit now in Australia, and a dose of medicine in France in the eighteenth century."[8] Recent logical discussions of identity and persistence through time are based upon the same ontological assumption.[9]

[7]See Franz Brentano, *Kategorienlehre* (Leipzig, 1933), p. 11: "Not only is every substance an entity [*ein Seiendes*] in the strict sense of the term, but so, too, is every plurality of substances and every part of a substance, as well as every accident." Cf. also *The True and the Evident* (London, 1966), p. 73. But in discussing theodicy, he said, "God and the world together do not constitute a thing; they are, rather, a multiplicity of things [*Gott und Welt zusammen sind kein Wesen, sondern eine Mehrheit von solchen*]" (*Religion und Philosophie* [Bern, 1954]), p. 176.

[8]J. E. M. McTaggart, *The Nature of Existence* (Cambridge, Eng., 1921), I, 141.

[9]One of the axioms of Lesniewski's mereology is this: "For every non-empty class a of individuals there exists exactly one individual x such that x is the *sum* of all the members of a." An "individual" x is said to be the *sum* of all the members of a class a provided (i) every member of a is a part of x and (ii) every part of x has a part in common with some member of a. Thus the conjunctive man would be such that every man is a part of it and every part of it shares a part with some man. On Lesniewski's mereology, see Eugene C. Luschei, *The Logical Systems of Lesniewski* (Amsterdam, 1962), pp. 149–53; Alfred Tarski, *Logic, Semantics, Metamathematics* (Oxford, 1956), pp. 24–29; and Appendix E (by Tarski) in J. H. Woodger, *The Axiomatic Method in Biology* (Cambridge, Eng., 1937). Cf. Henry S. Leonard and Nelson Goodman, "The Calculus of Individuals and its Uses," *Journal of Symbolic Logic*, V (1940), 44–55, and Rudolf Carnap, *Symbolic Logic* (New York, 1958), pp. 213–20.

W. V. Quine has recurred many times to the problem of Heraclitus and the river.[10] But like Brentano and McTaggart, he assumes (1) that there are sums of conjunctiva. Unlike Brentano, but like McTaggart, he also assumes (2) that individual things persisting through time, like their careers or histories, have "temporal parts." And unlike both Brentano and McTaggart, he assumes (3) that the temporal parts of individual things, also like the careers or histories of individual things, are "concrete *events*" or "*processes*," and therefore he does not hesitate to say that the temporal parts of a thing are "stages" of the thing. Combining these assumptions he says that "a physical thing— whether a river or a human body or a stone—is at any one moment a sum of simultaneous momentary states of spatially scattered atoms or other small physical constituents. Now just as the thing at a moment is a sum of these spatially small parts, so we may think of the thing over a period as a sum of the temporally small parts which are its successive states."[11] A river is thus a *process* through time, a sum of momentary "river stages." Quine suggests that this way of looking at the matter provides the solution to Heraclitus' problem. "The truth is that you *can* bathe in the same *river* twice, but not in the same river stage."[12]

We should note, however, that this way of looking at the matter, if it is thus to yield a solution to Heraclitus' problem, *presupposes* the concept of persistence through time—the concept of one and the same entity existing at different times. Even if it is true that all rivers are sums of river stages, it is not true that all sums of river stages are rivers. Indeed a sum of river stages occupying a continuous period of time need not be a river. Thus the Nile, from 9 to 10 A.M., Eastern Standard Time, the Mississippi from 10 to 11, and the Charles from 11 to 12, would be such a sum of river stages, occupying a three-hour period. But this particular sum, if there is such an entity, does not constitute a river.

What more is required for a sum of river stages to yield a river? Five possible answers suggest themselves. (1) We could say, of course, that river stages *a, b,* and *c,* occurring or existing

---

[10]These discussions go at least as far back as *O Sentido da Nova Lógica* (São Paulo, 1944), pp. 135–38, and continue in the works cited below and in *Word and Object*, pp. 114–18, 171–73.

[11]*Methods of Logic* (New York, 1959), p. 210.

[12]*From a Logical Point of View* (New York, 1963), p. 65.

at different times, are stages of the same river if and only if there is an x such that x is a river and such that a, b, and c are all stages of x. This answer, which is not very informative, obviously presupposes the concept of *a river* persisting through the time in question. (2) We could say that a, b, and c are all to be found in the same river bed, or between the same river banks.[13] But this would be to presuppose the concept of a *river bed*, or a pair of *river banks*, persisting through the time in question.

To be sure, we do not need to presuppose the concept of a persisting *physical thing* in order to say what sums of river stages make up rivers and what sums of river stages do not. Thus (3), given the concept of a *person* persisting through time, we might be able to define a persisting river in terms of river stages and accessibility to *his* observation. But in this case, presumably, we should not expect to define the persistence of a person by reference to the persistence of his body. Or (4), given the concept of a *place* persisting through time, we could say that a sum of river stages makes up a river provided its elements all occupy the same place. But then we should not expect to define the persistence of a place through time in terms of the persistence of the various physical things that might be said to occupy it. And presumably we should say, with Newton, that places are parts of space and that "absolute space, in its own nature, without relation to anything external, remains always similar and immovable."

Or, finally (5), we could introduce a technical term—"cofluvial" for example—and say that a, b, and c are stages of the same river if and only if they are *cofluvial* with each other.[14] But unless we

---

[13]This view is suggested by St. Thomas: "The Seine river is not 'this particular river' because of 'this flowing water,' but because of 'this source' and 'this bed,' and hence is always called the same river, although there may be other water flowing down it; likewise a people is the same, not because of sameness of soul or of man, but because of the same dwelling place, or rather because of the same laws and the same manner of living, as Aristotle says in III *Politica*" (*De Spiritualibus Creaturis*, Art. IX, ad. 16; *On Spiritual Creatures*, trans. M. C. Fitzpatrick and J. J. Wellmuth [Milwaukee, 1949], p. 109).

[14]This is the procedure that Quine follows, but instead of "cofluvial" he uses "river kinship." He writes: "We begin, let us imagine, with momentary things and their interrelations. One of these momentary things, called a, is a momentary stage of the river Caÿster, in Lydia, around 400 B.C. Another, called b, is a momentary stage of the Caÿster two days later.

have some independent way of explicating the concept of cofluviality, this fifth possible answer would seem not to differ substantially from the first.

For my own part, I am reluctant to count "sums" or "conjunctiva" as individual things. I would prefer to say, with Boethius, that a man and a horse are not one thing.[15] I think we *may* say, though we *need not* say, that those things that persist through time are made up of temporal parts. If we do say this, then we may construe the statement "St. Paul's had an interesting history during the nineteenth century" as referring to a certain entity which, like the history of St. Paul's, is such that part of it existed in 1801, another part of it existed in 1802, and so on, for all the other years of the century. But I am most reluctant to say that St. Paul's, like the history of St. Paul's, is *itself* a process or event. (It would certainly be a mistake—a "category mistake" if ever there was one—to say that St. Paul's *is* the history of St. Paul's.) With these preconceptions, then, let us consider the persistence of rivers, ships, and other such objects through time.

IV

To avoid mere verbal questions, let us introduce the technical term *"compositum"* to refer to what is made up of parts, and let us take the expression *"x is part of y"* as undefined but attempt to understand it in its ordinary sense.

Naturally the term "part," in its ordinary sense, is vague. It is very easy to think of borderline cases where we would not know whether to apply the term or not. For example, should we say of

---

A third, *c,* is a momentary stage, at this same latter date, of the same multiplicity of water molecules which were in the river at the time of *a*. Half of *c* is in the lower Caÿster valley, and the other half is to be found at diffuse points in the Aegean Sea. Thus, *a, b,* and *c* are three objects, variously related. We may say that *a* and *b* stand in the relation of river kinship, and that *a* and *c* stand in the relation of water kinship. Now the introduction of rivers as single entities, namely, processes or time-consuming objects, consists substantially in reading identity in place of river kinship" (*From a Logical Point of View*, p. 66). A more nearly accurate version of the final sentence would be: "The introduction of river stages as momentary entities consists substantially in reading river kinship in place of identity"—in place, that is, of a river that persists through time.

[15]See D. P. Henry, *The Logic of Saint Anselm* (Oxford, 1967), p. 56.

a card that had been part of a deck of cards that it is still a part of that deck of cards, once the various cards have been scattered or some of them torn apart? But there are also cases that are *not* borderline; let us confine ourselves to these. If we understand "part" in its ordinary sense, then it is clear that neither a man nor a fish should be called a part of a man and a fish. Nor should we call a fin or a foot a part of a man and a fish. But a foot is a part of a body of a man and a fin a part of a body of a fish.[16]

We may assume that the relation *part of* has the following three properties. (1) *Part of* is transitive: a part of a part of a thing is itself a part of the thing. If my thumb is a part of my hand and my hand is a part of my body, then my thumb is a part of my body. (2) *Part of* is also asymmetric: if A is part of B then B is not part of A. Nothing, then, will be a part of itself. Hence we are dealing with what mathematicians call "proper parts" and with what other people simply call "parts." And (3), everything that is a part of some thing is such that there is some other thing that is a part of it.[17]

We may say that a *compositum* is anything that has a part; in other words, if A is a compositum, then there is something B such that B is part of A. Let us consider a rather simple compositum, $UWXV$, made up of four building blocks, lettered "U," "W," "X," and "V," and fastened together in some way. The separate blocks, U, W, X, and V, are parts of this compositum. There is a clear sense in which we may say that these four blocks and *nothing else* are what make up this compositum; for it is composed of *just* these four blocks. Yet to say that it is composed of just these four blocks is *not* to say that these four blocks are the *only* parts of the compositum, for the blocks themselves have parts. Thus each block has a front half and a back half and these halves are themselves parts of the compositum $UWXV$. Moreover, although the compositum $UWXV$ is composed *just* of U, W, X, and V, it is *also* composed just of certain *other* things:

[16]I am assuming, then, that there is a reasonable mean between "monadism" and "collectivism"—where monadism is the view according to which there are no things composed of other things, and collectivism is the view according to which, for any two things A and B, there is a thing composed of just A and B.

[17]Cf. A. N. Whitehead's discussion of "part," in *The Organization of Thought* (London, 1917), pp. 158–66.

for example, UW and XV; also U, WX, and V; also U, W, X, and the right half of V and the left half of V; and so on. The blocks themselves make up smaller *composita* inside the larger *compositum*. Thus UW is a part of $UWXV$, and so are WX, UWX, XV, and WXV.[18] If, however, the blocks are laid along horizontally as in our picture, $UWXV$, then we should *not* say that UX, or UXV, or WV, or UVW are parts of $UWXV$. For these entities, if they *are* entities, are mere *conjunctiva* and are not joined together as *composita*. And this is quite in accord with our intuitions. My thumb is a part of my body; my hand, where this is construed as something that has the thumb and fingers as parts, is also *a* part of my body; but the *conjunctivum* consisting of my thumb and little finger is not also *a* part of my body.

What does it mean to say that our *compositum*, $UWXV$, is made up just of U, W, X, and V, or, as we may also say, *composed* just of U, W, X, and V? Let us note first that the separate blocks, U, W, X, and V, are entirely distinct from each other: they have no parts in common. And secondly, every part of $UWXV$ has some part in common either with U or with W or with X or with V. More generally, let us say:

> A is *entirely distinct* from B, provided: there is no X such that X is a part of A and X is also part of B.
>
> A is *composed of* B and C, provided: B is part of A; C is part of A; B is entirely distinct from C; and there is no part of A that is entirely distinct both from B and from C.[19]

And now we may make one negative point about identity. If we say that the chair *is* the back, the seat, and the legs, we are not using the "is" of identity. We are using what has been called *"the 'is' of composition."* We are saying that the back, the seat,

---

[18]Cf. McTaggart: "Great Britain, for example, consists of England, Scotland, and Wales. And it does not consist of anything except England, Scotland, and Wales. But these are not all the parts of Great Britain, for Surrey is also a part of it" (*The Nature of Existence*, I, 134).

[19]These definitions (in a somewhat different terminology) were suggested by Whitehead, *The Organization of Thought*, pp. 159–60. If we wish to accommodate the first definition to the possibility that there are simples (a possibility which, in fact, is precluded by our third assumption about the relation *part of*), we should add the further clause "it is false that A is identical with B"; otherwise, the definition would require us to say of any simple that it is entirely distinct from itself.

and the legs are what make up the chair—that the chair is *composed of* the back, the seat, and the legs, in the sense of "composed of" just discussed.[20]

Before returning to our puzzles, let us consider certain relevant things that may happen to composita, or certain things that may be done to composita.

We may remove a part, say U, from our compositum and there will be two resulting composita, WXV and U, which no longer go to make up a single compositum. In such a case, we may say that $UWXV$ has been disassembled. (Or should we say just "partially disassembled"? But "partially disassemble" contrasts with "completely disassemble." And can one completely disassemble anything, if we are right in assuming that for each part of a thing there is something that is a proper part of that part?) Using tenseless language, we might define the relevant concept of disassembly in the following way:

> A is *disassembled* at t, provided: there is an X and a Y such that A is composed of X and Y at a time prior to t, and nothing is composed of X and Y at t.

(In our example, A would be $UWXV$, X would be U, and Y could be WXV.) But if we take tense seriously, we will prefer to say:

> A has been *disassembled*, provided: there was an X and a Y such that A had been composed of X and Y, and nothing is composed of X and Y.

In this latter case, presumably we should also say that A has been *destroyed*, that it has *ceased to be*. (And this is why we say "there was" rather than "there is" in the definiens, since X and Y may have been disassembled, too.) Hence there is this significant difference between our composition $UWXV$ and the conjunctivum or sum made up of just U, W, X, and V: in separating U from

[20]U. T. Place has used the expression "the 'is' of composition," and cites the following as examples of its use: "her hat is a bundle of straw tied together with string," "a cloud is a mass of water droplets or other particles in suspension." But he understands the expression somewhat more broadly than it is intended here, for he says that the "is" in "consciousness is just brain process" is the "is" of composition. See U. T. Place, "Is Consciousness a Brain-Process?," *British Journal of Psychology*, XLVII (1956), 44–50.

WXV, we destroy the compositum, but we do not destroy the conjunctivum or sum.[21]

We may also *rearrange* the parts of a compositum with disassembling it, and therefore without destroying it. Provided we don't allow any one of the four blocks to be separated from all the others, we may rearrange our compositum *UWXV* by putting our blocks in the order *VUWX* instead of *UWXV*. But, although the total compositum *UWXV* has not been disassembled in this process, some of those composita that go to make up *UWXV* have been disassembled, namely, *XV* and *WXV*. (If disassembling a compositum is the same as destroying it, these facts are relevant to what one might call "the theory of destruction." The fact that we can rearrange the parts of a compositum without destroying it may lead us to believe, mistakenly, that we may confine our activities to rearrangement without ever destroying anything.)

Let us now picture a child playing with lettered blocks of the kind we have been discussing. He can fasten them together and take them apart; he makes horizontal composita and then alters them in various ways, for whatever reasons you may care to imagine. Let us suppose that he starts with four blocks, *W, E, C,* and *A*. Perhaps he has found them already fastened together, left over from the previous day. Starting with this compositum, he creates what I would like to call an "evolving system of composita." One such system is illustrated by the accompanying diagram.

(1) WECA
(2) WEC
(3) WECI
(4) WICE
(5) WECI

These various composita, each of the lower ones being made from the one immediately above it, exemplify various types of change. Thus, from (1) to (2), we have mere removal, or subtraction, of a certain part. The child simply separates *A* from *WEC*, thus disassembling and therefore destroying *WECA*. In the change from (2) to (3), we have addition. The child adds *I* to *WEC*,

<hr>

[21]This is not to say, of course, that conjunctiva or sums are incapable of destruction.

thus causing *WECI* to come into being. In the change from (3) to (4), we have mere rearrangement (provided the child does not separate any of the blocks from the others). And in the change from (4) to (5), we also have rearrangement, but this time, some may be tempted to say, rearrangement that involves "re-creation." For if (5) is the *same* compositum as (3), then the creation of (5) was tantamount to the re-creation of (3).[22]

Our child, with his building blocks, could supply us with a model of a river. Were he to construct the system depicted by the accompanying diagram, we could see that new blocks are ever flowing in and old ones flowing out.

WXYZ
VWXY
UVWX
TUVW
STUV
RSTU
QRST
PQRS

In stepping into *the same river* twice, one first steps into one compositum of water molecules and then one steps later into

[22]But *is* (5) the same compositum as (3)? In creating (5), *did* the child bring (3) back into being? Or did he simply create a compositum having the same parts as (3) and having them in the same order? Thomas Reid said: "That which hath ceased to exist, cannot be the same with that which afterwards begins to exist; for this would be to suppose a being to exist after it ceased to exist, and to have had existence before it was produced, which are manifest contradictions. Continued uninterrupted existence is therefore necessarily implied in identity" (*Essays on the Intellectual Powers of Man,* essay III, chap. 4, in *Works,* p. 344). Cf. Locke's "One thing cannot have two beginnings of existence" in Book II, chap. xxvii, sec. 1, of his *Essay.* Reid's argument seems to be fallacious, however. It *is* a manifest contradiction to say of a thing that it "had existence before its *first* production" or that it will "have existence after its *final* passing away." But to assume that a thing's production must be its first production and that its passing away must be its final passing away is to beg the question at issue and thus to presuppose rather than to prove that a being cannot begin to exist after it has ceased to exist. The horror of Nietzsche's doctrine of eternal recurrence, for many of us, lies in the fact that it implies that we—we, ourselves—will come into being an infinite number of times and cease to exist, or pass away, an infinite number of times. And my own feeling is that it is neither contradictory nor senseless to suppose that a person may come into being again after he has ceased to exist.

is a logical construction. It has been decreed, let us suppose, that the U.S.S. South Dakota is the aluminum ship compositum. So now all of us, or those of us who conform, call the aluminum compositum "the U.S.S. South Dakota"; it will continue the traditions that were established in the wooden compositum, and the captain now knows where his obligations lie. But everything that we know about the U.S.S. South Dakota *could* be put by reference merely to the different composita which at different times went to make it up. Talk about ships that endure through time can be reduced to talk about composita, to talk about evolving systems of composita, in just the way in which talk about the average Englishman can be reduced to talk about particular Englishmen. We may say that the U.S.S. South Dakota had a long and glorious history, but this is *not* to say that in addition to the wooden composita, the mixed ones, and the aluminum ones, there was *also* a ship that had a history. Similarly, we may say that the average Englishman has 0.7 cats in his house, but this is not to say that in addition to particular Englishmen, cats, and houses, there is an average Englishman who has in *his* house 0.7 of a cat.

Or, if we do not care for the modern terminology, we may say that the ship, like Aristotle's musical man, is an *"ens per accidense."*[27] The ship is "an accident" of the various composita that served to make it up. We have seen that the ship need not survive the evolving series of composita that, for a while, served to make it up. The ship will cease to be, once the series becomes a system of composita serving to make up a house on land. Now surely when, as we say, the ship "ceases to be," what has happened is simply that the system of composita has been *altered*. Some compositum that served to make up a ship evolved into a compositum that did not make up a ship, and this compositum in turn evolved into one that made up a house.

What I have said about ships holds in principle for most of the familiar physical things that we encounter—rivers, chairs, trees, picket lines. I would suggest that most physical things are similarly reducible to evolving systems of composita. The particular thing, as St. Augustine said, is "composed of many, all

[27]"The musical man passed away and an unmusical man came to be, but the man persists as identically the same" (*Generation and Corruption*, I, 4, 319b).

of which exist not together."[28] I have considered only fairly simple ways in which composita may evolve into other composita. The relations among actual evolving systems may be much more complex.

Railroad trains provide an interesting example. Consider the late "Phoebe Snow," which left Hoboken every morning for Chicago.[29] The cars were substantial enough. But two trains of cars—two composita made up by attaching cars together—could both go to make up the "Phoebe Snow" without the one in any way evolving from the other. Today's train did not need to have any cars in common with yesterday's, but it had to keep the same schedule and travel over the same roadbed, or rather it had to keep approximately the same schedule and travel over approximately the same roadbed. Had you pointed in the direction of the train and asked, "Have you ever ridden on that?" your question might well have been ambiguous, depending upon what you meant to single out with your use of "that." You might have meant simply the "Phoebe Snow"; you might, if you were a trainman, have meant that particular train of cars or, more likely, just that particular car; or you might, had you been Heraclitus, have meant that particular compositum which at that particular moment went to make up that particular car or train of cars.

But the increase in complexity of these various composita and their interrelations makes no difference to the two general points I wanted to stress: the one being that our criteria for what it is for two composita to make up the same so-and-so are defeasible and a matter only of convention (it makes no sense to say that our altered criteria are incorrect, false, or mistaken); and the other point being that familiar physical things may be regarded either as "logical constructions upon," or as "accidents of," what I have been calling "evolving systems of composita."

VI

What, then, is the point of speaking of a "loose and popular" sense of identity?

---

[28]*Confessions,* IV, xi.

[29]Alternative ways of looking at passing away are reflected in two different headlines announcing its demise: "Phoebe Snow Rolls into Oblivion" (*Providence Evening Bulletin,* Nov. 28, 1966) and "Phoebe Snow Runs Will End on Nov. 27" (*New York Times,* Nov. 13, 1966).

Let us return to the problem of identifying ships through time. The accompanying diagram illustrates, very schematically, what might occur.

A
B
C   D
E   F

A, we may suppose, was the compositum that was originally launched. It evolved into *B*; *B* then evolved into two distinct composita, *C* and *D*; *C* then evolved into *E*; and *D* evolved into *F*. Suppose now we find two reasonable men disputing about *E* and *F*, where, as in our diagram, *E* is to the left of *F*. The one man says, "The ship on the left is identical with the ship that we traveled on when we took the maiden voyage, and the ship on the right is not." The other man, feeling himself in strong disagreement, says, "That is entirely wrong. The ship on the right is identical with the ship that we traveled on when we took the maiden voyage, and the ship on the left is not." What are we to say of these uses of "is identical with"?

The following relevant points seem to me to be clear. (1) Compositum *E* is not identical with compositum *F*; (2) compositum *E* is not identical with compositum *A*; (3) compositum *F* is not identical with compositum *A*; (4) *E* and *A* belong to a system of composita, namely *ABCE*, to which *F* does not belong; (5) *F* and *A* belong to a system of composita, namely *ABDF*, to which *E* does not belong; (6) both *E* and *F* belong to a system of composita, namely *ABCDEF*, to which *A* belongs; and (7) *A* belongs to a system of composita, namely *AB*, to which neither *E* nor *F* belongs.

If our two men can be made to see these points, then, since we have assumed them to be reasonable, perhaps they will agree that their dispute over the question "Is the ship on the right, or the ship on the left, identical with the ship that we traveled on when we took the maiden voyage?" is a dispute merely about words and one that can be settled merely by agreeing upon a set of conventions. If their dispute concerned any of the points, (1) through (7) above, it would be a dispute about the strict and philosophical sense of identity. But if they agree on points (1) through (7), then they are disputing only about the loose and popular sense of identity.

VII

And what now of Bishop Butler's second thesis—his thesis that it is in a strict and philosophical sense and not merely in a loose and popular sense that we can speak of the persistence of one and the same *person* through time? This thesis might be construed as telling us that there is a very clear sense in which the concept of sameness, or identity, as applied to persons persisting through time, is *not* subject to "defeat" or to "convention"—that there is a very clear sense in which, so far as "defeat" and "convention" are concerned, "the same person" differs fundamentally from "the same ship," "the same house," and "the same railroad train."

Now there is, of course, a sense in which the concept of "the same person" *is* subject to defeat and *is* at the mercy of convention. What I wish to say is that the persisting person differs from the persisting ship in that there is *also* a sense in which the applicability of "same" is *not* subject to defeat or at the mercy of convention.

But let us first note the sense in which this concept *might* be subject to defeat in order that we may contrast it with the sense in which it is not. There are circumstances under which one might say, "Mr. Jones is not at all the same person he used to be. You will be disappointed. He is not the person that you remember." We would not say this sort of thing if Mr. Jones had changed only slightly. We would say it only if he had undergone changes that were quite basic and thoroughgoing—the kind of changes that might be produced by psychoanalysis, or by a lobotomy, or by a series of personal tragedies. But just *how* basic and thoroughgoing must these changes be if we are to say of Mr. Jones that he is a different person? The proper answer would seem to be "As basic and thoroughgoing as you would like. It's just a matter of convention. It all depends upon how widely it is convenient for you to construe the expression 'He's the same person he used to be.' In so far as the rules of language are in your own hands, you may have it any way you would like."

But this is only a "loose and popular" sense of identity. When we say, in this sense, "Jones is no longer the person he used to be," we do not mean that there is, or was, a certain entity such that Jones was formerly identical with that entity and is no longer so. We do not mean to imply that there are (or have been) certain entities, x and y, such that at one time x is, or was, identical with y, and at another time x is not identical with y. For this, I believe, is incoherent, but "Jones is no longer the person he used to be" is not.

Nor do we mean, when we say, "Jones is no longer the person he used to be," that there *was* a certain entity, the old Jones, which no longer exists, and that there is a certain *different* entity, the new Jones, which somehow has taken his place. We are not describing the kind of change that takes place when one president succeeds another. In the latter case, there is a clear answer to the question "What happened to the old one?" The answer might be "He was shot" or "He retired to Gettysburg." But when we decide to call Jones a new person, we are not confronted with such questions as "What happened, then, to the old Jones? Did he die, or was he annihilated, or disassembled, or did he retire to some other place?"

For the old Jones did not die; he was not annihilated or disassembled and he did not retire to any other place. He *became* the new Jones. To say of anything that it became a so-and-so is to say of it that it took on certain properties that it did not have before. (But contrast the "became" of "Jones then became a married man," said when Jones ceased to be a bachelor, with that of "The President then became a Democrat," said when President Eisenhower retired.) When we say of a thing that *it* has properties that *it* did not have before, we are saying that there is an x such that x formerly had such-and-such properties and x presently has such-and-such other properties. But to say that there is an x—at least one x—such that x was this and x is now that, is to presuppose the identity of x through time, in the "strict and philosophical" sense of identity. So if we say that Jones is "not the same person" he was before, we are using "same" only in a "loose and popular" sense; but in saying that *he* is not the same person that *he* was before, we are presupposing that, in the "strict and philosophical" sense, the same person has in fact persisted from then until now.

"But," one may object, "*need* we presuppose this? Need we presuppose the persistence of a single subject of change when, as we say, the man becomes 'a new person'?" To appreciate the situation, it may be necessary to imagine that the person in question is oneself. Suppose, then, that you were such a person, that you had undergone basic and thoroughgoing changes, and that your friends and acquaintances were in agreement that you are no longer the same person that you were.

What if you *remember* all of the relevant facts, that *you* had formerly been a person of such-and-such a sort, that you had undergone certain shattering experiences, and that these then led to a transformation in your personality, with the result that you are not the person that *you* formerly were?

Let us imagine, however, that your friends and acquaintances say to you: "But you are such a *very* different person now that henceforth we are going to treat you like one. We will call you 'Smith' instead of 'Jones.' We will make certain that you are free from all the obligations that Jones incurred. And if you feel guilty about some of the wicked things that Jones did, you need no longer do so. For we can get the highest courts to lay it down that you are two quite different people." Something, surely, is wrong here.

Some people, I have found, see at once that something is wrong and others do not. For those who do not, let me propose that we look in a different direction. What would we think of such talk if we were to hear it *before* rather than after the transformation of our personality?

It will be instructive to elaborate upon an example that C. S. Peirce suggests.[30] Let us assume that you are about to undergo an operation and that you still have a decision to make. The utilities involved are, first, financial—you wish to avoid any needless expense—and, secondly, the avoidance of pain, the avoidance, however, just of *your* pain, for pain that is other than yours, let

---

[30] "'If the power to remember dies with the material body, has the question of any single person's future life after death any particular interest for him?' As you put the question, it is not whether the matter ought rationally to have an interest but whether as a fact it has; and perhaps this is the proper question, trusting as it seems to do, rather to instinct than to reason. Now if we had a drug which would abolish memory for a while, and you were going to be cut for the stone, suppose the surgeon were to say, 'You will suffer damnably, but I will administer this drug so that you during the suffering lose all memory of your previous life. Now you have of course no particular interest in your suffering as long as you will not remember your present and past life, you know, have you?'" (*Collected Papers* [Cambridge, Mass., 1935], V, 355).

us assume, is of no concern whatever to you. The doctor proposes two operating procedures—one a very expensive procedure in which you will be subjected to total anesthesia and no pain will be felt at all, and the other of a rather different sort. The second operation will be very inexpensive indeed; there will be no anesthesia at all and therefore there will be excruciating pain. But the doctor will give you two drugs: first, a drug just before the operation which will induce complete amnesia, so that while you are on the table you will have no memory whatever of your present life; and, secondly, just after the agony is over, a drug that will make you completely forget everything that happened on the table. The question is: given the utilities involved, namely, the avoidance of needless expense and the avoidance of pain that *you* will feel, other pains not mattering, is it reasonable to opt for the less expensive operation?

It seems to me quite obvious that it is *not* reasonable, even if you can be completely certain that the two amnesia injections will be successful. It will be *you* who undergoes that pain, even though you, Jones, will not know that it is Jones who is undergoing it and even though you will never remember it. But although this seems quite obvious to me, I must concede that I cannot supply you with an *argument* for it. I am afraid I can say only that either you see it or you don't.

Now I can appreciate that it might not seem obvious to you, as you ponder your decision. You *may* say to yourself: "I would certainly like to save the money. But I wonder—won't it be I who's going to feel the pain, won't *I* be in agony, even if I don't know that it's I?" I can understand your not being sure and I can appreciate that what is here obvious to me may not be obvious to you. But there is a slightly different point that *ought* to be obvious to you, and if this other point is not obvious I am afraid I will not appreciate it. Suppose that others come to you as you ponder your decision—friends, relatives, judges, clergymen. And they say: "Have no fear. Take the cheaper operation and we will take care of everything. We will lay it down that the man on the table is not you, Jones, but is Smith. We will not allow this occasion to be mentioned in your biography. And during the time that you lie there on the table—excuse us (they will interject), we mean to say, during the time that *Smith* lies there on the table —we will say 'Poor Smith' and we will not say, even in our hearts, 'Poor Jones.'" What *ought* to be obvious to you, it seems to me, is that the laying down of this convention should have no effect at all upon your decision.

Suppose you knew that your body, like that of an amoeba, would one day undergo fission and that you would go off, so to speak, in two different directions. Suppose you also knew, somehow, that the one who went off to the left would experience the most wretched of lives and that the one who went off to the right would experience a life of great happiness and value. It seems to me, first, that there is no possibility whatever that *you* would be *both* the person on the right and the person on the left. It seems to me, secondly, that there *is* a possibility that you would be one or the other of those two persons. I think, moreover, that *you* could be one of those persons and yet have no memory at all of your present existence.[31] It follows that it would be reasonable of you to hope that you will be the one on the right and not the one on the left, also that it would be reasonable of you to have this hope even if you knew that the one on the right would have no memory of your present existence. Indeed it would be reasonable of you to have it even if you knew that the one on the *left* thought he remembered the facts of your present existence. And it seems to me to be absolutely certain that no fears that you might have, about being the half on the left, could reasonably be allayed by the adoption of a convention, even though it were laid down by the highest authorities.

[31]In this case, there might well be no *criterion* by means of which you or anyone else could decide which of the two halves was in fact yourself. I would agree with Shoemaker's contention that "our ability to know first-person psychological statements to be true, or the fact that we make them (for the most part) only when they are true, cannot possibly be explained on the supposition that we make them on the basis of criteria" (*Self-Knowledge and Self-Identity*, p. 214). It follows from this contention, I think, that it makes sense to suppose, in connection with the above example, that you are in fact the half that goes off to the left and not the one that goes off to the right even though there is no criterion at all by means of which anyone could decide the matter. I would disagree, incidentally, with what Shoemaker says (pp. 236ff.) about the relationship between criteria and necessary truths—at least, if "necessary" is taken to mean the same as "logically necessary." My own views on this question may be suggested by chapter IV ("The Problem of the Criterion") in my *Theory of Knowledge* (Englewood Cliffs, N.J., 1966).

Comments

SYDNEY S. SHOEMAKER

Professor Chisholm's paper defends the view of Bishop Butler that the identity we ascribe to ships and the like is identity only in a "loose and popular sense," whereas the identity ascribed to persons is identity in a "strict and philosophical sense." This is a view I have a good deal of sympathy with, and I think that until we have satisfactorily explained the considerations that make it plausible we cannot claim to have an adequate understanding of the way in which the notion of identity applies to familiar kinds of things, and in particular to persons. A number of these considerations, including some that hitherto have gone virtually unnoticed, are brought out extremely well in Chisholm's paper. But it is my present opinion that explaining the plausibility of Butler's view must, in the end, amount mainly to explaining it away. There are interesting and important differences between the identity of persons and the identity of other things, but I do not believe that these differences are aptly described by saying that only the former is identity in the "strict and philosophical sense."

I shall comment first on what Chisholm says about the identity of ships and other sorts of physical things. One of his claims is that ships and the like may be regarded as "logical constructions upon," or as "accidents of," what he calls "evolving systems of composita." The contrasting claim about personal identity, which Chisholm does not explicitly argue in this paper, is that persons are *not* logical constructions. I agree that persons are not logical constructions, but I find some difficulties in the thesis that ships are logical constructions.

Presumably part of what is meant by saying that ships are logical constructions upon evolving systems of composita is that it is not merely true but necessarily true that if a ship existing at t_2 is identical with a ship that previously existed at t_1 then there is an evolving system of composita satisfying a certain description, one member of which existed at t_1 and another member of which exists at t_2. Now this may be true, but is it clear that it is necessarily true? One difficulty, which I will pass over quickly, is that Chisholm's explication of the notion of a compositum, or of the notion of a part in terms of which the notion of a compositum is defined, seems to assume the infinite divisibility of matter. For he tells us that "everything that is a part of a thing is itself something that has a part." The difficulty I see here is simply that it seems unclear what are to count as the parts of a ship when we get down to the submicroscopic level, and that if it is said that the parts are the elementary particles of physical theory then we cannot rule out a priori that the best theory will turn out to be one according to which the elementary particles are extensionless and so do not themselves have parts.

Let us waive this difficulty, though, and assume that at any time at which a volume of space is occupied by a ship it is occupied by a compositum, which we will call a "ship compositum." Even on this assumption it does not seem to me clearly necessary that the different ship composita that constitute the ship at different times should form an evolving system of composita in Chisholm's sense. Suppose that a ship is in the harbor all day, but that at noon one ship compositum ceases to exist there and another takes its place. For the later of these ship composita to have directly evolved from the earlier it is necessary that they have parts in common. But is this necessary in order for it to be the case that the ship in the harbor after noon is the same as the one that was there before? It seems to me conceivable, though it is perhaps quite unlikely, that the best physical theory should turn out to be one according to which there is constant "creation" and "annihilation" of particles at the submicroscopic level, each fundamental particle existing for only a billionth of a second. If we may speak of these fundamental particles as the "ultimate parts" of all composita, it might then be the case that the last ship compositum in the harbor before noon should have no ultimate parts in common with the first ship compositum in the harbor after noon, even though the case is one in which anyone would say that there had been one and only one ship in the harbor all day long. It may be said that while these two temporally adjacent ship composita would have no *ultimate* parts in common, they would still have parts in common, e.g., planks, and that this is enough to satisfy the condition that the later of them directly evolved from the earlier. But it would appear that, on Chisholm's account, these ship composita can have planks in common only if they have parts of planks in common, that they can have parts of planks in common only if they have parts of parts of planks in common, and so on until we get down to the ultimate parts. And so it would seem that if they have no ultimate parts in common they can have no parts in common at all, and that the later of them cannot have directly evolved from the earlier. Yet it seems to me very clear that the acceptance of such a physical theory would not lead us to say that for all we know there is a different ship in the harbor every minute or so.

I turn now to a different point. The way in which Chisholm originally introduces the expression "compositum" makes it appear that ordinary physical things, ships, tables, automobiles, etc., are composita, for such things are composed of the very sorts of parts of which composita are said to be composed. Yet Chisholm tells us that "in stepping onto the same ship twice, one steps first onto one compositum and then steps onto what in all probability is another compositum." The identity conditions for ships differ from the identity conditions for composita. The ship now in the harbor cannot be said to be, in the sense of being identical with, the ship compositum now in the harbor, for things will be true of the former, e.g., that it was built ten years ago and that I stepped onto it yesterday, that are not true of the latter.[1] And this gives rise to difficulties.

First of all, while it is clear enough what are to count as parts of a ship, it now begins to be unclear what are to count as the parts of the composita that somehow constitute the ship. A plank

---

[1]Here I am relying on Leibniz's law of "the indiscernibility of identicals." In his recent paper "Time, Existence and Identity" (*Proceedings of the Aristotelian Society,* 1965–66), A. N. Prior has suggested that we may have to abandon this law in order to be able to apply the notion of identity to cases of "fission" (such as that mentioned by Chisholm at the end of his paper). But Prior points out that if we abandon this law we will still have the law *"CIxyCIxzAAIyzPIyzFIyz,"* which says: "If x is identical with y then if x is identical with z then either y is identical with z or y has been identical with z or y will be identical with z." And this law is sufficient to yield the result that a ship cannot be identical with each of the different composita that constitute it.

can be part of a ship, but can a compositum have a plank as a part? It seems that planks, like ships, will turn out to be not composita but "logical constructions upon evolving systems of composita." In that case the ship compositum will presumably be composed not of planks, but of plank composita. And is it clear what these are, and what their parts will be? The difficulty here is that Chisholm's account relies on our ordinary understanding of "part," "composed of," etc. in its explanation of the notion of a compositum, and yet tells us, by implication, that what we would ordinarily count as things composed of parts are not composita and that what we would ordinarily count as the physical parts of things are not the parts of which composita are composed.

A further difficulty is that Chisholm's procedure at one point seems to require him to say that ships are composita, or rather that some composita are ships. He says that if Noah Webster's definition of "ship" were satisfactory we could say of two composita, A and N, that they make up or constitute the same ship if the following condition holds: "A is (or was) a structure used for transportation in water and so is N; and each compositum B such that B evolved from A and N evolved from B was also a structure used for transportation in water." But this involves speaking of the individual ship composita as "structures used for transportation in water," and in Webster's definition this would mean that the composita are ships. It is true that Chisholm goes on to say that Webster's definition is unsatisfactory, but it looks as if the procedure he outlines for defining "same ship" depends on the definition of "ship," whatever it is, applying to the different composita that constitute the same ship at different times. Now there is of course nothing wrong with different ϕ's constituting the same ψ. Different bricks make up a single building, and those who don't object to speaking of rivers as four-dimensional entities can say with Quine that the same river is built up out of different river stages. But while there is no objection to speaking of one and the same ship being constituted out of different something-or-others, there does seem to be something wrong with saying that the different something-or-others that constitute a ship are themselves *ships*.

Someone might try to avoid these difficulties by taking the Geachian line that "x is the same as y" is always elliptical for something of the form "x is the same F as y," where F occupies the place of a general term. He could then say that the compositum in the harbor today and the one that was there yesterday are both ships, and that while they are different *composita* they are one and the same *ship*. But this seems to me a very questionable view.[2] It is true that a sentence of the form "*x* is the same as *y*" will not express a definite statement unless the reference of its terms is clear, and that one common way of making the reference of the terms clear is by inserting a general term after "same." But that, I think, is the only function such a general term can serve there; it seems to me a mistake to think that the general term can have the function of indicating that one sort of identity rather than another (ship identity rather than compositum identity, or vice versa) is being asserted to hold between already specified entities. There are not, I think, different sorts of numerical identity, though there can be identity statements about indefinitely many kinds of entities. It is worth noting that the insertion of a general term after "same" is not the only way of making the reference of the terms of an identity statement clear. The sentence "What you see in the harbor is the same as what you saw in the harbor yesterday" can be said to be elliptical, for the phrase "what you see in the harbor" can refer to, among other things, either a ship or a ship compositum. But the sentence "The ship in the harbor is the same as the ship that was in the harbor yesterday" is not elliptical and does not require the insertion of a general term after "same."

If what I have been saying is right, Chisholm cannot assume that the individual composita that constitute a ship will satisfy the definition of "ship," and he needs some other way of specifying these composita if he is to make out his claim that ships can be regarded as logical constructions upon evolving systems of composita.

I turn now to Chisholm's other claim about such things as ships, namely that the criteria for the identity of such things are "defeasible and a matter only of convention," and his claim that this constitutes a difference between the identity of such things and the identity of persons. I shall begin with a truism or two. First of all, there is a familiar sense in which the meaning of any word whatever is a matter of convention. And since what counts as

[2]Some of the difficulties in it have been very ably brought out in an unpublished paper by John Perry.

being the same ϕ is always determined at least in part by the meaning of the word "ϕ," there is a sense in which all criteria of identity are conventional. If "person" meant what is in fact meant by "ship," the criteria for the identity of what then would be called "persons" would obviously be different from the criteria for the identity of what are now called "persons." But also, there is no word that is immune to change in meaning. And since, again, the meaning of a word determines, at least in part, the identity conditions for the things to which the word applies, there is a sense, a rather trivial and uninteresting one, in which all criteria of identity are "defeasible" in the sense of being alterable by convention. All of this applies just as much to the word "person" as to any other word. Since it seems unlikely that Chisholm would disagree with what I have just said, it would appear that he must have in mind conventions other than those that determine the meanings of the terms "ship" and "person" when he says that the criteria of ship identity are "a matter only of convention" and denies that this is true of the criteria of personal identity.

It seems to me that the truth value of statements about the identity of such things as ships sometimes is and sometimes is not determined in part by conventions that can be changed without changing, or changing significantly, the meanings of the expressions involved. Consider the sentence "The building Jones is in is the same as the building Smith is in." And suppose, to begin with, that Jones and Smith are situated just as Professor Chisholm and I are situated at present. Here, I think, the empirical facts together with the meanings of the terms in that sentence determine that the statement expressed by the sentence is true. Given the facts and the meanings of the terms, there is no room for the operation of any other convention in determining the truth value of the statement. The only way of "defeating" this identity statement, given the facts, is by changing the meaning of the word "building" or of some other word or words. In this sense we can also "defeat" any statement of personal identity. But of course it is misleading to say that one is defeating a statement if what one is doing is changing the meaning of a sentence so that instead of expressing that statement it expresses a different statement that is false. Consider, however, a different sort of case: Suppose that Jones is in Alpha Hall and Smith is in Beta

Hall, and that Alpha Hall and Beta Hall are joined at some point so that it is possible to get from one to the other without being rained on. Here I am inclined to say that the facts together with the meanings of the words "building," "same," etc. do not by themselves determine the truth value of the statement. If we had been in the practice of saying in such cases that the people were in different buildings, and if for some reason we altered our practice, I would be hesitant about saying that we had changed the meaning of the word "building." Here there seems to be room for the operation of conventions other than those that define the meanings of the words, or at any rate conventions that can be changed without significantly altering the meanings of the words. It is such conventions as these that I will call "defeasible."

In the cases just considered, the identity asserted is what might be called "identity through space" rather than identity through time. It may be Chisholm's view that all statements asserting the identity of a physical thing through time are like my second example of an assertion of identity through space rather than like my first example, i.e., are such that their truth values depend on defeasible conventions. But I do not believe that this view is correct. Consider the statement "The building we are now in is the same as the building we were in when Professor Chisholm began to read his paper." Anyone who knew the facts and seriously disputed this statement would thereby be convicted of lack of understanding of one or more of the expressions in the sentence used to make the statement. And if we all changed our practice of making identity statements so that in cases like this we would say that the building we are in now is numerically different from the one we were in half an hour ago, I think this would have to be described as a change, and a fairly substantial change, in the meaning of the word "building," or in the meanings of other words. But there certainly are cases in which the empirical facts together with the meanings of words do not unequivocally determine the truth value of statements asserting identity through time; Chisholm's example of the U.S.S. South Dakota seems to me such a case. And I think that the conventions determining the truth value of statements asserting identity through time are more often defeasible—or, if defeasibility can be made a matter of degree, are typically more defeasible—than those governing the truth conditions of statements asserting identity through space. The reasons for this are interesting, but I do not have the space to go into them here.[3] In any case, Chisholm is certainly right in thinking that some of the conventions governing the truth conditions of identity statements about such things as ships and buildings are defeasible conventions.

I have not been operating here with anything like a theory about "sameness of meaning" or a criterion for saying whether the

[3]Very briefly, I think this has to do with the fact that when "ϕ" is a word like "ship," or "building," the ability we regard as most central to knowing the meaning of "ϕ" is the ability to identify or classify things as ϕ's and distinguish ϕ's from non-ϕ's. Having this ability typically involves knowing a good deal about how something must be distributed in space in order to be a ϕ—since size and shape will be prominent among the features by which things are classified as falling under such concepts— and it therefore involves knowing, at least for a large class of cases, the truth conditions of statements of the form "The ϕ at place p and the ϕ at place p' are one and the same." But, while something's being correctly classifiable as a building depends on its being distributed in space in a certain way, it does not depend in any comparable way on how the thing is distributed in time. What "temporal size" something has (i.e., how long it exists) has little to do with whether it is correctly said to be a building. And, as Judith Thomson has pointed out (in "Time, Space and Objects," *Mind*, January, 1965), if we introduce a notion of temporal shape that parallels our ordinary notion of spatial shape, it turns out that the temporal shapes of things play no role in our classifications of them into kinds. Hence knowledge of the truth conditions of statements of the form "The ϕ at t and the ϕ at t' are one and the same" does not play the central role in classification and identification that is played by knowledge of the truth conditions of statements of the form "The ϕ at place p and the ϕ at place p' are one and the same."

What I have said of course gives no answer to the deeper question of why we classify things in such a way that there is this asymmetry between identity through space and identity through time, which I think is much the same as the question of why we operate with an ontology, or conceptual scheme, in which the basic particulars, to use Strawson's term, are three-dimensional objects rather than four-dimensional objects. I think that this has to do in part with the difficulty of applying the four-dimensional view to persons.

For discussions relevant to the points touched on here, see Michael Woods's "Identity and Individuation" in *Analytical Philosophy*, ed. R. J. Butler (2d series; Oxford, 1965) and the paper by Judith Thomson mentioned above.

meaning of a word has changed "significantly." I have simply been following my vague intuitions regarding these notions, one of which is that it would not be natural to say that British judges mean something different by "ship" from what American judges mean simply because, what is imaginable, British courts rule that the wooden ship is the U.S.S. South Dakota while American courts rule that the aluminum ship is the U.S.S. South Dakota. And it does seem to me that it must be at least part of what Chisholm means in calling the criteria of ship identity "defeasible" that they rest on conventions that we can change without significantly altering the meaning of the word "ship." For, as I have been insisting, if a change of convention that alters identity conditions by changing the meaning of a word is allowed to count as "defeating" a criterion of identity, the criteria of personal identity will be as defeasible as any others.

Now I think, with certain qualifications that I shall make later, that it is by and large true that the criteria of personal identity differ from those of ship identity in not being defeasible and alterable by convention. At first I thought that this is because the concept of a person is to a considerable extent defined, or constituted, by the criteria of personal identity, and that for this reason any attempt to make a substantial change in these criteria is likely to succeed only in changing the meaning of the word "person," i.e., making it express a different concept from what it does now. The suggestion is that the criteria of personal identity are much more central to the concept of a person than are the criteria of ship identity to the concept of a ship, and that this accounts for the difference Butler and Chisholm see. But while I still think that this is part of the story, I do not think that it is the whole of it. Part of the difference, I think, consists in, or is accounted for by, a difference between the kind of *interest* we have in personal identity and the kind we have in the identity of other sorts of things. Chisholm says at one point that part of what is meant by saying that the criteria of ship identity are defeasible is that "we reserve to ourselves the right of revising these criteria should they turn out to sanction uses that would be inconvenient or otherwise undesirable." This recognizes the important fact that identity judgments have social consequences, which we may or may not find to be in accord with our interests. What we need to understand is why it is that judgments of ship identity can have consequences that are undesirable in such a way as to make it reasonable to change the criteria of ship identity and thereby avoid having to make such judgments, whereas this does not seem to be true in the case of personal identity.

Both identity judgments about persons and identity judgments about other things have social consequences. It is the car that is judged to be identical with the one I bought last year that I am now regarded as having a legally enforceable right to use pretty much as I choose, and it is the person who is judged to be identical with the person who bought that car who now is regarded as having such a right to its use. And, of course, it is the person who is judged to be identical with the person who committed the crime last year who will now be punished for it. But our interest in personal identity is not related to our interest in the social consequences of judgments of personal identity in the same way as our interest in the identity of such things as cars and ships is related to our interest in the social consequences of identity judgments about them. Suppose that I am concerned, as indeed I am, that my car, the one I have now, be in good condition tomorrow. I may, of course, have a sentimental attachment to my car, but my primary interest is in being the beneficiary tomorrow of the social consequences of the general acceptance of a judgment to the effect that a car then in good condition is identical with the car I have now and so belongs to me—the desired consequence is my having at my disposal tomorrow a car in good condition. Here I might say, oversimplifying just a bit, "I don't care which car of tomorrow is judged to be identical with this one, as long as it is in good condition." But compare this with my concern that *I* be in good condition tomorrow, that I be healthy, prosperous, and happy. Here it would seem absurd to say, "I don't care which self of tomorrow is judged to be identical with me, as long as that self is healthy, prosperous and happy." And while I certainly am not indifferent to the social consequences of the identity judgments I expect to be made about me tomorrow, it is not at all because of these consequences that I have concern for my future welfare. I am inclined to say, "What I want is not that the self of tomorrow who is judged to be me, or who is counted as being me, should be healthy, prosperous, and happy, but that the self of tomorrow who *is* me should be healthy, prosperous, and happy."

This bears on Chisholm's ingenious and intriguing elaboration of Peirce's operation example. You will recall that it is proposed to someone that we prevent him from suffering the pain of an operation by modifying the criteria of personal identity in such a way that the person who suffers the pain will not count as him, i.e., will not count the same as the person who had the same body before and after the operation. A natural response to this remarkable proposal would be to say, "Look, what I am interested in is not whether the person who suffers the pain is going to be *called* me, or *counted as* me, or *regarded as* me; what I am interested in is whether he will *be* me." One would not be likely to make a corresponding distinction between one's interest in whether the car that will be damaged tomorrow will be counted or regarded as identical with one's present car and one's interest in whether the damaged car will *be* identical with one's present car. And this difference may seem to lend support to the view that the identity of such things as cars is conventional in the sense that whatever is generally counted as being the same car *is* being the same car, while personal identity is not conventional in this sense.

What we need to clarify is the nature of the interest we have in personal identity, and in particular the nature of the special concern that each of us has for his own future welfare. So far I have made about this only the negative point that this interest is quite unlike the interest we have in the identity of things *qua* items of property. In trying to understand the nature of this concern for future welfare, and its relation to the concept of personal identity, it is helpful to try to imagine people whose attitudes toward their future selves is different from our own. To this end I shall, with apologies, ask you to consider an imaginary tribe.

The members of my imaginary tribe are, with one important difference, like us only more selfish: they are thoroughgoing rational egoists who have concern for the welfare of others only when they think this affects their own welfare. The important exception is this: at all times except during the twilight hours the members of this tribe are completely indifferent to what their own welfare will be during the twilight hours, except as they view this as affecting their welfare at other times, and each member of the tribe shows (except during the twilight hours) a concern for the welfare during the twilight hours of some other member of the tribe, say the neighbor who lives on his right, this concern being exactly like the concern he has for his own welfare at other times. If a member of the tribe finds (during the nontwilight hours) that others are preparing to torture him when twilight falls, he shows no fear and makes no attempt to prevent this, unless he thinks that the torture will cause him pain or bodily damage that will last past the twilight hours; if, however, he finds that people are preparing to torture his right-hand neighbor when twilight falls, he makes every effort to prevent this, and if he is unsuccessful he shows increasing fear as twilight approaches. Members of the tribe who have to undergo operations attempt to schedule them during the twilight hours, so as to avoid the cost of anesthesia, though of course their left-hand neighbors try to prevent this. And each member of the tribe attempts to make provisions to insure that his right-hand neighbor is provided with food and drink, and other pleasures, during the twilight hours—though in doing this he is faced with the difficulty that if he makes his right-hand neighbor a gift prior to twilight his neighbor is likely to pass on the gift to *his* right-hand neighbor. I am imagining that these attitudes are as natural to these people as any of our attitudes are to us, and that no amount of argument will persuade any of them that it is not simply incredible that during the nontwilight hours he should have any concern, except perhaps a general humanitarian concern, for his own welfare during the twilight hours.

The first observation I would like to make about this example is that it does not seem to me right to say that the members of this imaginary tribe would be unreasonable or irrational. Granted, their conduct will seem irrational if judged by our standards of rationality, but I can see no sense in applying our standards of rationality to creatures who are as different from us as these creatures are imagined to be. And after all, it is not as if we have reasons for saying that our standards of rationality are themselves rational. Given what my imaginary people naturally want and strive for, I think they would not be misusing the word "rational" if they described someone as rational if he passed up some present good in order to provide a greater good for his right-hand neighbor during the twilight hours, and if they described someone else as irrational because by some shortsighted action he made it possible for himself to avoid being exploited by his neighbor during the twilight hours.[4]

The second observation I would like to make is that there is a sense in which the people in my imaginary tribe do not regard their twilight-hour selves as really being themselves. I shall not try to argue this; as Chisholm says about something else, either you see it or you don't. If you accept it you will perhaps agree with me that having a special regard for the welfare of a future self is *part* of what it *is* to regard that self as oneself. Wittgenstein suggested, if I understand him, that the "belief" that others have souls is at least partly a matter of having a certain sort of attitude toward others. I am making a similar suggestion, and I am afraid a similarly vague suggestion, about first-person beliefs in personal identity.

A third observation, following upon the last one, is that if my imaginary tribe started off using our criteria of personal identity —let us take these to be bodily continuity and continuity of memory—it would not be surprising if they elected to change these criteria somewhat so as to bring their judgments of personal identity into line with their attitudes, i.e., so as to permit them to say that at twilight a man "becomes," takes over the body and memories of, his right-hand neighbor. For obvious reasons the social consequences of judgments of personal identity made in accordance with *our* criteria of personal identity would often be unacceptable to my imaginary people; for one thing, they would prefer that during the twilight hours each man should have a legally enforceable right to the use of goods acquired by his left-hand neighbor at other times. Of course, instead of changing their criteria of personal identity they might change their insti-

---

[4]There is one difficulty here. We would not ordinarily allow that a man had acted rationally if he knew, or should have known, that he would subsequently regret his action. Yet the members of my tribe regularly do things that they know that they will regret during the twilight hours. But I think that the sense in which these people regret their previous actions during the twilight hours is not quite our ordinary sense of "regret." For such regretting will not involve the man's thinking that his previous actions involved a mistake, or miscalculation, or shortsightedness, or weakness of will, nor will it involve resolving to behave differently in the future— for the members of the tribe know that resolves formed during the twilight hours have no effect on their behavior at other times.

tutions of property and punishment so that judgments of personal identity would have different social consequences. Which they would do, I suppose, would depend on which they regarded as more central to the notion of personal identity: its connections with the notions of bodily continuity and memory, or its connections with such notions as that of moral responsibility and that of a right to the possession and use of something. It does not seem to me that there is any clear sense in which they could be said to be *mistaken* in making either of these changes, or in which they could be mistaken in making one of the changes (in the criteria, or in the institutions) rather than the other. If I understand Chisholm's position, he would disagree with me about this and would say that the question whether a man in the twilight hours would be the same as the man who at other times has the same body must have a correct answer that is independent of whatever conventions these people adopt, and that this is so whether or not it is possible to determine what that correct answer is.

What I have tried to imagine in describing this hypothetical tribe is a case in which there is a breakdown in a correlation that with us is fairly constant—a correlation between, on the one hand, a person X having at time t a special concern for the welfare of person Y at a later time t', and, on the other, its being the case, or X's believing it to be the case, that our ordinary criteria of personal identity would give the verdict that person X at t and person Y at t' are one and the same person. The final point I wish to make about this example is that it is essential to its intelligibility that the imagined breakdown in this correlation is a fairly limited one. What it is not possible to imagine, I believe, is a tribe each member of which never shows any concern for his own future welfare, or for what our usual criteria of personal identity would require us to call his future welfare, but does show a concern for the future welfare of some other member of the tribe.

I have not the space to show in detail how an attempt to give a coherent description of such a tribe would break down, but several points should be noted. First, I think that to have no regard for one's future welfare would amount to having no concern for one's welfare at all. The future is continuous with the present, and even trying to get rid of a pain one now has is showing concern for one's future welfare. If we try to imagine that these people never behave in ways that show concern for their future welfare, we will have to imagine that they never behave in ways that show that they find something pleasant or unpleasant. This already calls into question the claim that it is *people* one is imagining. But also, if there is nothing the people in this tribe find pleasant or unpleasant, nothing they want to get and keep for themselves, then the notion of *welfare* seems to have no application to them, and in that case it cannot after all be part of the description of the case that each member of the tribe has a concern for the future welfare of some other member of the tribe. It is also worth noting that such notions as that of *fear* would have no application to the members of this tribe, for fear as we know it is a primitive form of concern for one's own future welfare. I think that such considerations as these show that if we try to describe a set of people whose behavior does not show concern for their own future welfare, or what would be judged to be their future welfare on the basis of our present criteria of personal identity, we will find that nothing in their behavior can show concern for anyone, and that what we have described cannot be called people at all. It is, I think, not merely true but conceptually true that there are close connections between personal identity, as judged by our usual criteria, and the various attitudes and emotions I have been calling "special concern for future welfare." The connection between these perhaps need not be as tight as it is with us, i.e., the subject of the special concern perhaps need not invariably be identical with the person who is its object, but I think we cannot describe a case in which it is systematically absent without significantly changing the meaning of the word "person."

In this connection it is worth noticing a connection between having concern for one's future welfare and having the sort of memory knowledge each of us has of his own past. Concern for one's future welfare is manifested in purposive activity, which typically occurs over a period of time and involves the performance of sequences of actions that stand in complex means-ends relationships to one another, and only a creature who has memory knowledge of its own past, including its own past intentions, could engage in such behavior. One difficulty that would be faced by the members of the imaginary tribe I described earlier is that during the twilight hours a man would have no memory knowledge of the past actions and intentions of his left-hand neighbor, and so would be hampered in his attempts to carry to completion enterprises that his neighbor had initiated in his behalf. If we try to imagine a general breakdown in the correlation between remembering the actions and intentions of a past self and being the self for whose welfare that past self had special concern, we have to imagine the absence of the very sort of purposive behavior in which this concern ought to manifest itself.

Now let us try to see how all this applies to Chisholm's claim that in its application to persons, as contrasted with its application to other things, the concept of identity is not subject to convention. I have already suggested that there are conceivable circumstances in which it would be understandable if people adopted a convention that would enable them to decide questions of personal identity differently from ways they had done this in the past. This would be so if, as in the case of my imaginary tribe, the future selves that they had special concern for were frequently not the future selves their old criteria of identity would require them to speak of as their future selves, and if as a result of this the social consequences of identity judgments made on the basis of those criteria were less acceptable to them than would be the social consequences of identity judgments based on some altered set of criteria. But of course our actual situation is not at all like this. The future selves we have special concern for *are* the future selves that our criteria of identity require us to regard as ourselves, and I have suggested that we run into conceptual difficulties if we try to imagine people who are *very* different from us in this respect. Our judgments of personal identity are already in line with our attitudes, so there is no need for a convention that brings them into line. Of course, a change in the criteria of personal identity might be to the advantage of a few individuals, e.g., it might enable someone to escape punishment for a crime. But if there is any truth in the claims made for justice, and for the practices that dictate the social consequences of judgments of personal identity, such a change would not produce consequences that would be acceptable to people in general. One true thing that can be meant by the claim that the criteria of personal identity are not alterable by convention is that, given our interests and attitudes, and given the social consequences of judgments of personal identity, any change in the criteria that made a difference would be a change for the worse. This can be viewed as a moral point. Ships and automobiles have no interests, and we are free to treat them as means and to alter their criteria of identity as suits our convenience. But unless we are willing to treat persons as mere things, we cannot change the criteria of personal identity without taking into account the interest of persons in general, and I think that if we take these interests properly into account any change that would make a difference will be ruled out.

One way of expressing the point I have been trying to make is by saying that if possible our criteria of personal identity ought to be such as to make true the proposition "The future selves that people have a direct and special concern for are the future selves they regard as themselves." But this is not the only proposition our criteria ought to make true. Suppose that a proposed criterion of personal identity gave the verdict that actions I remember doing—or, if you like, seem to remember doing—usually were done by someone other than myself, and that intentions I form are usually carried out by someone other than myself. Assuming that other criteria are available that do not have these bizarre consequences, I think we could say that the proposed new criterion would not be a criterion of *personal* identity at all, and that anyone who insisted on applying the expression "same person" on the basis of it would simply have changed the meaning of the word "person." Part of acquiring the concept of a person is learning the use of the first-person pronouns, and learning the use of these pronouns is inseparable from learning to make a wide variety of first-person statements—memory statements, statements of intention, statements expressing desire and fear, and so on. The concepts of such forward-looking and backward-looking mental states as fear, desire, intention, memory, and regret all involve the concept of personal identity, and I think that acquiring these concepts involves coming to accept as true such propositions as: "If what a person fears happens, it is usually that person who is harmed," "If a person decides to do something, and what he decides to do gets done as the result of his decision, then (generally) it is that person who does it," and "'If a person seems to remember doing a past action of a certain description as the result of someone's having done an action of that description, he is identical with the person who did the action." Perhaps none of these propositions is by itself straightforwardly analytic or logically necessary. But I think that such propositions as these, and the proposition that persons have special concern for their own future welfare, are constitutive of the concept of a person at least in the sense that they provide a standard of acceptability for criteria of personal identity. The best set of criteria would be one that made all of these propositions true, and if some set of criteria satisfies this condition then any other competing set of criteria, any set that makes one or more of these propositions false, can on that account be rejected. If this is right then we can perhaps say that the reason why the criteria of personal identity are not alterable by convention is simply that our actual criteria conform to this standard and any revision of them is for that reason ruled out.

The fact that our actual criteria satisfy this standard of acceptability consists in part in the fact that they permit us, i.e., make it true, to characterize persons as creatures that have a special sort of knowledge of their own identities. It is characteristic of certain kinds of first-person statements that while they imply statements of personal identity, or at any rate imply the persistence of a person through time, they are not normally grounded on criteria of identity. I have argued at length elsewhere that this is true of first-person memory reports.[5] And it seems clearly true of statements of intention; it seems obvious that my statement that I will go to a concert this evening does not rest on my having identified as myself, by means of criteria of identity, someone who will go to the concert. But, while such statements are not grounded on criteria, they can be judged to be true or false (by others, or by ourselves in retrospect) on the basis of criteria; and a person's ability to learn to make such statements—and to have the sorts of knowledge they express—consists mainly in the fact that he can be taught, or trained, to make statements that are not grounded on criteria of identity and yet are for the most part true if judged by our present criteria of identity. And whereas people are in fact such that they can be trained to make, without using criteria, statements about themselves that conform to our present criteria, they are not such that they can learn to make, without using criteria, statements that conform to criteria that conflict with our present criteria. We

[5] See my *Self-Knowledge and Self-Identity* (Ithaca, N.Y., 1963), esp. chap. 4.

can imagine people (or creatures) who can be taught to make, without using criteria, first-person judgments that conform to criteria of identity that are wildly incompatible with ours, but such people would be very different from ourselves. Given the way persons in fact are, only our present criteria of personal identity permit us to ascribe to persons an important sort of self-knowledge, and this is one reason why these criteria do not strike us as arbitrary or as subject to change, although the fact that having this self-knowledge involves knowing one's own identity without using these criteria (or any others) makes it appear that personal identity transcends its criteria.

But what of cases, such as Chisholm's fission example, where our present criteria of personal identity do not seem to decide questions of personal identity? I am not as convinced as Chisholm is that if my body were to undergo fission it is out of the question that I would be both the person who goes off to the right and the person who goes off to the left.[6] But this is too complicated a question to be examined here. In any case, I agree with Chisholm that in such cases it would be unreasonable to let one's hopes and fears concerning one's own future welfare be influenced by the adoption, even by the highest authorities, of a convention determining the application of the concept of identity to persons. I said earlier that our criteria of identity ought to be such as to make true the proposition "The future selves that people naturally have a direct and special concern for the welfare of are the future selves they regard as themselves." But I think that making this proposition true has got to consist in bringing our criteria in line with our attitudes of concern rather than bringing our attitudes of concern in line with some arbitrarily adopted convention or criterion. Our attitudes of concern are simply not modifiable in this way by the adoption of conventions governing the truth conditions of statements, and if someone's attitudes were modifiable in this way I would want to say either that he was confused—e.g., that he was confusedly treating a convention as if it were a statement of fact—or else that he was psychologically so different from us that our standards of rationality and reasonableness would not apply to him.

There is one thing that puzzles me about Chisholm's position.

[6]For a defense of the view that this is not out of the question, see A. N. Prior, " 'Opposite Number,' " *Review of Metaphysics,* 1957, and "Time, Existence and Identity."

The force of much of what he says at the end of his paper rests on the fact that it is one's own future welfare that is the primary focus of one's hopes and fears, and I think he takes it for granted that we have, and that it is natural and reasonable for us to have, a special kind of concern for our own future welfare that we do not have for the future welfare of others. But does he regard this as an analytic truth or as a synthetic truth? If he thinks that it is a synthetic truth, it is not clear to me why he is so confident that it would hold in circumstances, such as his fission case, that are vastly different from any we have encountered or have any like-lihood of encountering. Supposing that I could be persuaded, by considerations having to do with the transitivity of identity, that it is quite impossible that both products of the fission of my body will be me, it is not clear that it would be unreasonable for me to say, "Still and all, I feel an equal concern, and a concern of the same kind, for the welfare of both these future persons; I view with fear and dread the sufferings of the one, and at the same time I view with delighted anticipation the rich and happy life of the other." To be sure, there does seem something logically peculiar about saying that one *dreads,* or views with delighted *anticipation,* a future happening in which one believes that one will not oneself be involved. And this may suggest that it is a logical or analytic truth, rather than a synthetic truth, that the object of one's special concern for future welfare (of which dread and delighted anticipation are determinate forms) has to be one's own future welfare. But I am not sure that it is open to Chisholm to hold this. The claim that this is an analytic truth might be sup-ported by arguments, of the sort sketched earlier, to show that there are conceptual connections between concern for future wel-fare and the empirically discoverable relationships, such as bodily continuity and continuity of memory, that we use as criteria of personal identity. But Chisholm, if I understand him, thinks that the relationship between personal identity and these criteria is a synthetic one, and on this view it would not follow from there being an analytic relationship between special concern for future welfare and our usual criteria of personal identity that there is an analytic relationship between special concern for future welfare and personal identity itself. If one holds, as I think Bishop Butler did, that personal identity consists in an unanalyzable substantial unity that is only synthetically connected with any of our usual criteria of personal identity, it is difficult to see how it could be analytically true that people have, or that it is reasonable for them to have, a special concern for their own future welfare. Indeed, it is hard for me to see why on *that* view it should be true at all that one should be concerned about one's future welfare when, as must be possible on that view, the future delights and sufferings are not linked to one's "present self" by our present criteria of personal identity. Here I am inclined to side with Leibniz, who wrote the following in his *Discourse on Metaphysics* (XXXIV) : "Suppose that some individual could suddenly become King of China on condition, however, of forgetting what he had been, as though being born again, would it not amount to the same practically, or as far as the effects could be perceived, as if the individual were annihilated, and a King of China were at the same instant created in his place? The individual would have no reason to desire this."

Reply

RODERICK M. CHISHOLM

I

Mr. Shoemaker's careful and penetrating observations indicate that there are many respects in which my paper requires clarification and correction. As a result of his criticisms, I feel far more clear about the problems involved than I had before. But I also feel that the fundamental theses of the paper, which I had attributed to Bishop Butler, are sound and that Shoemaker has not succeeded in "explaining them away."

I cannot do justice to everything he has said. I shall consider just his more serious criticisms, first as they apply to what I said about nonpersons, and secondly as they apply to what I said about persons.

II

To deal with the questions Shoemaker raises about "evolving composita," let us use the following diagram to schematize the history of the U.S.S. South Dakota:

V	Z	i	Z	i	j	i	j	i	j	i	j
W Y		W Y		W Y		k Y		k l		k l	
X		X		X		X		X		m	
(a)		(b)		(c)		(d)		(e)		(f)	

We may suppose that a is the compositum of the first day; one part is replaced, so that on the second day a "directly evolves" into b; and so on, with the result that compositum f of the sixth day, though it has "indirectly evolved" from a, has no parts in common with a. But though the compositum of the sixth day is thus different from the compositum of the first day, and from those of the other four days, we may yet say that the ship of the sixth day is identical with the ship of the first day and with that of the other four days: the U.S.S. South Dakota has persisted all along. One of Shoemaker's questions may now be put as "Should we say that these six different composita are themselves ships?"

Let us agree, for simplicity, that Webster has provided us with an acceptable definition of "a ship": x is a ship, we may say, if and only if x is used for transportation in water. And let us assume that each of the six composita depicted above is (or was) used for transportation in water. It will follow, therefore, that each of six composita is a ship. And so, as Shoemaker points out, we are now confronted with a philosophical problem. The problem might be summarized by asking: "How are we going to be able to say consistently that each of the six different composita is a ship and yet that there is only one ship, only one U.S.S. South Dakota? And how are we going to be able to say consistently that though the ship of the first day is identical with the ship of the sixth day, the compositum that constitutes the ship of the first day is not identical with the compositum that constitutes the ship of the sixth day?"

Our definition of "x is a ship" allows us to say that each of our six composita is a ship. We need a definition of "x constitutes the same ship as does y" which will allow us to say that our six different composita, our six different ships, constitute the same ship. Hence the definition of our second concept should not imply "x is identical with y" since the six composita that constitute the same ship are not identical with each other. Nor should the definition imply "x is diverse from y" since we want to be able to say, after all, that x constitutes the same ship as does y.

(Finding an acceptable definition of "x is a ship" is a problem for dictionary-makers. Their definition, if it is not merely a description of how certain people at a certain time use the expression "is a ship," will be a convention, and like any such convention it will be subject to revision. Finding an acceptable definition of "x constitutes the same ship as does y" is more likely to be a problem for jurists. Their decision will be a decree and, like any such decree, will be subject to defeat. Both types of definition might be called "conventions," but they are conventions of rather different sorts. Shoemaker remarks, correctly, that "Chisholm . . . must have in mind conventions other than those that determine the meanings of the terms 'ship' and 'person' when he says that the criteria of ship identity are 'a matter only of convention'

and denies that this is true of the criteria of personal identity."
I was concerned with the conventions involved in "x constitutes
the same ship as does y" and "x constitutes the same person as
does y," and not with those involved in "x is a ship" and "x is
a person." But I was not sufficiently clear about the distinction.
It is quite possible for people to agree about a definition of "x is
a ship" while disagreeing about "x constitutes the same ship as
does y," or to agree about the latter and to disagree about the
former. Shoemaker is right in saying that "it would not be natural to say that British judges mean something different by 'ship'
from what American judges mean simply because, what is imaginable, British courts rule that the wooden ship is the U.S.S.
South Dakota while American courts rule that the aluminum ship
is the U.S.S. South Dakota." In the situation imagined, the two
courts have the same interpretation of "x is a ship" and different
interpretations of "x constitutes the same ship as does y.")

I had proposed in my paper a definition of "x constitutes the
same ship as does y." So far as our actual usage is concerned,
the definition is oversimplified. Let us ignore this oversimplifica-
tion for the moment (just as we are ignoring the fact that Webster's definition of "ship" is oversimplified), for I wish to suggest
that the definition gives us a kind of "model" which will enable
us better to understand the problem of the ship of Theseus and
of the U.S.S. South Dakota. The definition may be put as
follows:

> x constitutes at t the same ship that y constitutes at t', pro-
> vided only: x is a ship at t, y is a ship at t', and every z such
> that z evolves from x and y evolves from z, or such that z
> evolves from y and x evolves from z, is also a ship.[1]

The definition allows for the possibility that x is diverse from
y; it also allows for the possibility that x is identical with y.[2]

Given this definition of "constituting the same ship," we may
now define what it is to constitute the U.S.S. South Dakota:

[1] The original definition, however, lacked the clause beginning with "or"
and used Webster's definiens in place of "a ship." To avoid the problem of
fission (the problem of having to say of two ships that they are both the
U.S.S. South Dakota at one and the same time), we might want to add
to the above: "No such z directly evolves into more than one ship."

[2] In defining what it is to say that one compositum "evolves" from another, I had said: "For simplicity, let us misuse the term 'evolves' so that
we may also say that any given compositum evolves from itself."

x constitutes the U.S.S. South Dakota at *t*, provided only:
x is a ship at *t*, and everything that constitutes the same ship
that *x* constitutes at *t* is a U.S.S. South Dakota.

This definition may be said to presuppose that "U.S.S. South
Dakota," when taken in a strict and philosophical sense, is a
generic name.[3] The name may apply to more than one thing but
not to more than one thing at a time; and if it applies to two
things, one of them must have evolved from the other. (If the
lady who christens the ship were to speak in a strict and philosophical sense, she would say: "I hereby christen everything that
constitutes the same ship as you do 'U.S.S. South Dakota.' ")

Some of the things that are true of the U.S.S. South Dakota
are true of the particular composita that constitute it; thus if *a*
is grey and 400 feet long on the first day, so is the U.S.S. South
Dakota. And some of the things that are true of the U.S.S. South
Dakota are not true of the particular composita that make it up;
thus the U.S.S. South Dakota endures for six days, but each of
its composita endures for only one. But those true statements in
which something is predicated of the U.S.S. South Dakota that
may not be predicated of any of its composita may be paraphrased
into true statements in which something is predicated of its composita. This is what I meant when I said that the U.S.S. South
Dakota is a "logical construction" upon its composita. To say
that the U.S.S. South Dakota persisted from Sunday through
Friday, for example, will be to say something like this: There
was a compositum which was a ship and a U.S.S. South Dakota
on Monday, and there is a compositum which constitutes on Friday the same ship which that compositum constituted on Monday.

With this "model" in mind, let us now attempt to deal with
the kind of difficulties Shoemaker has called attention to. When
we say, in connection with the composita of our example, "There
are six different ships," we are speaking in what Bishop Butler
would call a strict and philosophical sense. But when we say,
"There is only one ship," we are speaking in what he would call
a loose and popular sense. A more strict and philosophical formu-

---

[3]Cf. Hume: "Tho' we commonly be able to distinguish pretty exactly
betwixt numerical and specific identity, yet it sometimes happens that we
confound them, and in our thinking and reasoning employ the one for the
other" (*A Treatise of Human Nature*, Book I, Part IV, sec. vi ["Of Personal Identity"], Selby-Bigge edition, pp. 257–58).

lation of the second statement would be: "There is a set of things all constituting the same ship." Therefore the first of our two statements does not contradict the second.

When we say, "The ship which is the U.S.S. South Dakota on the first day is not identical with the ship which is the U.S.S. South Dakota on the sixth day," we are speaking again in what Butler would call a strict and philosophical sense. But when we say, "The ship that is the U.S.S. South Dakota on the first day is identical with the ship that is the U.S.S. South Dakota on the sixth day," we are speaking in what he would call a loose and popular sense. A more strict and philosophical formulation of the second statement would be: "The ship that constitutes the U.S.S. South Dakota on the first day constitutes the same ship as does the ship that constitutes the U.S.S. South Dakota on the sixth day." Therefore, once again, the first statement does not contradict the second.

And when we say, "The ship that is the U.S.S. South Dakota on the first day persisted for only a day," we are speaking in the same strict and philosophical sense. But when we say, "The ship that is the U.S.S. South Dakota on the first day persisted for six days," we are speaking in the loose and popular sense. A more strict and philosophical formulation would be: "There is something x that constitutes the U.S.S. South Dakota on the sixth day and there is (or was) something y that constitutes on the first day the same ship that x constitutes on the sixth day." And so here, too, the first of our two statements does not contradict the second.

Hume said we have a "propensity" to "substitute the notion of identity, instead of that of related objects."[4] In application to ships, his point might be put by saying that we have a propensity to substitute the notion of one ship for that of related objects constituting the same ship. Using language in a loose and popular sense, we say things that are true—but things that would be false if our terms were taken in a strict and philosophical sense. Then, becoming philosophical, or semiphilosophical, we try to take these things in their strict and philosophical sense and we then encounter contradictions.

I would say, therefore, that the way to treat the problem of the

[4]*Ibid.*, p. 254.

ship of Theseus and that of the U.S.S. South Dakota (and the other puzzles I mentioned at the beginning of my original paper) is to note such things as these.[5]

It should be emphasized that, in saying of the various uses just discussed that they are loose and popular rather than strict and philosophical, I am not suggesting that they are *incorrect*. Indeed, they may be said to be correct, for it is the loose and popular interpretation rather than the strict and philosophical one that gives us the standard of correctness (at any rate, in the loose and popular sense of "correctness").

III

The adequacy of the foregoing account of the problem of the ship of Theseus will depend upon the adequacy of our definitions, in particular of "x is a ship" and of "x constitutes at t the same ship that y constitutes at t'." These are admittedly over-simple. I feel certain, however, that the refinements needed to make them adequate would not affect in principle what we have said. The problems involved in defining "x is a ship" are surely immaterial. And there is room for substantial revision of the definition of "x constitutes the same ship that y does" just so long as we continue to take it in such a way that it implies "x is a ship and y is a ship" and does not imply "x is identical with y" or "x is diverse from y."

The proposed definition, or criterion, of "x constitutes at t the same ship that y constitutes at t'" presupposes the persistence of *some* entity through *some* period of time, in the strict and philosophical sense. That is to say, it presupposes that there is some x which is such that we can say "x at t is identical with x at t'," where "is identical with" is taken in the strict and philosophical sense. For the definition makes use of the concept of "evolves"; but in order for one compositum to evolve from another, I had said, it must evolve directly from something, and in order for one compositum to evolve directly from another the two com-

---

[5]In answer to other questions that Shoemaker raises, I would say that it is possible for a compositum to be a ship, for the compositum like the ship to have planks among its parts, and for these planks in turn to be themselves composita. I would defend this answer in much the way I have attempted to deal with the problems above.

posita must "have some parts in common." In other words, if
N at t' directly evolves from A at t, where t' is later than t, then
there is something x such that x was part of A at t and x is part
of N at t'.

It may well be, as Shoemaker suggests, that the concept of
identity of ships through time is even looser than I had suggested.
Conceivably, he says, all the "ultimate parts" of a ship may be
annihilated at a certain moment and then, a very, very short time
later all of them replaced by parts that then came into being *ex
nihilo*.[6] In this case the two composita would have no parts in
common and therefore the later one cannot have evolved from the
earlier. "Yet," he observes, "it seems to me very clear that the
acceptance of such a physical theory would not lead us to say
that for all we know there is a different ship in the harbor every
minute or so." I would venture to say, though, that if in such a
case we *are* justified in saying that the ship that is in the harbor
now is the same as the one that was there a moment ago, it is
because of the persistence of *some* x through time in the strict
and philosophical sense—some x such that x at one time can be
said to be identical, in the strict and philosophical sense, with x
at another time. We must say either: (1) that some other physical thing, e.g., the harbor, or the dock, or the buildings on the
dock, evolved in the way that I suggested, so that with each step
of evolution some part persists through it; or (2) that portions
of absolute space, if there is such an entity, persisted through time
(and this would enable us to secure the identity of physical things
by reference to their relation to persisting places); or (3) some
observer, some *person* who has been observing the various physical things involved, has persisted in the strict and philosophical
sense through time. But if there is no such strict persistence of

---

[6]Shoemaker notes that my account presupposes the infinite divisibility
of matter and observes that "we cannot rule out a priori that the best theory will turn out to be one according to which the elementary particles
are extensionless and so do not themselves have parts." I will not attempt
to do justice to this objection. But I would say (1) that we can rule out
a priori the possibility of arriving at something unextended merely by divid-
ing up things that are extended, and (2) that if "the best theory" tells us
that "the elementary particles are extensionless," then the relation of these
particles to that of the macroscopic objects with which we are familiar is
not that of part to whole.

any of these entities, then, I think, it would make no sense to refer to the identity of a material thing through time.

IV

I turn now to Shoemaker's observations about the identity of persons through time. He has convinced me that there was at least one mistake involved in my speculations about the possibility of fission. I had said this: If you know that your body will undergo fission, that the person who goes off to the right will lead a life of happiness, and that the person who goes off to the left will not, then it will be reasonable of you to hope that you will be the one on the right and not the one on the left. But I agree with Shoemaker's suggestion that the one hope is, as such, really no more reasonable than the other. Instead of saying, "It will be reasonable of you to hope that you will be the one on the right," I should have said, *"If* you have a more special concern for the future welfare of yourself than for that of any other person, *then* it would be reasonable to hope that you will be the one on the right."[7]

But I am more reluctant to accept Shoemaker's positive observations about such "special concern." It is sometimes said that there are "two main competing answers" to the question "What are the criteria for the identity of a person through time?," one being that "the criterion of the identity of a person is the identity of the body which he has," and the other being that "the criterion of the identity of a person is the set of memories which he has."[8] For purposes of abbreviation, we might call these "the bodily criterion" and "the memory criterion," respectively. Shoemaker, as I interpret him, is now proposing a third, which we might refer to as "the special concern criterion."

He writes: "Having a special regard for the welfare of a future self is *part* of what it *is* to regard that self as oneself." Certainly

---

[7]Or, more accurately: "It would be unreasonable for a man, at one and the same time, both (1) to have a more special concern for his own future welfare than for that of anyone else, and also (2) to have no concern, in the situation imagined, about the possibility that he might be the one that goes off to the left."

[8]See Terence Penelhum's article, "Personal Identity," in *The Encyclopedia of Philosophy,* ed. Paul Edwards (New York, 1967), VI.

such regard is a fairly good *sign* of what one takes one's future self to be. If we find, for example, that Mr. Nixon's plans for 1970 are all directed toward the comfort and well-being of the man he believes will then occupy the White House, we might do well to infer that he thinks that he himself will be that person. But surely we should not *identify* (1) making a man the object of one's special concern and (2) regarding that man as being oneself.

What then could we say of mothers, martyrs, patriots, willing slaves, family retainers, and all those other people who, according to common belief, take as the object of their special concern the well-being of *others*—the well-being of persons they *know* to be other than themselves? If we accept Shoemaker's criterion, should we say of these people that they are not as altruistic and "self-less" as we had thought? Should we say that they think they really *are* those people, or that they are going to *become* those people, for whom they are now making what *we* think of (mistakenly?) as being sacrifices? (If we must answer these questions affirmatively, then the refutation of "psychological egoism" will be far less simple than most of us now think that it is.)

To understand Shoemaker's suggestion, let us consider the imaginary tribe he depicts. He tells us, it will be recalled, that "each member of the tribe shows (except during the twilight hours) a concern for the welfare during the twilight hours of some *other* member of the tribe, say the neighbor who lives on his right, this concern being exactly like the concern he has for *his own welfare* at other times" (my italics). Given what Shoemaker says about the "special concern" criterion, I am not entirely certain how we are to understand this suggestion. There are two rather different possibilities.

Consider at most two members of this tribe. Shoemaker's language suggests that he is envisaging the following situation:

(A) There exists an x and a y such that: x is a person who lives on the left side and not on the right, y is a person who lives on the right side and not on the left, and during the day x devotes his special concern to the nocturnal welfare of y.

We may say, of the situation described by (A), that in the strict and philosophical sense the x and y involved are different persons. For (A) logically entails "x is not identical with y" and therefore, in the strict and philosophical sense, "x is not the same person as y." And so if x and the other members of his tribe think that x "changes his identity" at night, they are simply deluded.

But I think that the situation we are to imagine is more complex. Let us consider this alternative:

(B) There exists an x, a y, a z, and a w such that: x is a person, y is a person, z is a body that is housed day and night on the right side and not on the left, w is a body that is housed day and night on the left side and not on the right, z is the body of x during the day, w is the body of y during the night, and the object of x's special concern during the day is the nocturnal welfare of y.

If the "special concern" criterion is adequate, then (B), taken literally, would imply that a most extraordinary event has taken place. For it would imply that sometime during the twilight hours, between day and night, z ceased to be the body of x, and w began to be the body of x. What kind of happening was this? Did x transmigrate from z to w, and if so how fast did he go? Or did he cease to be, while z was his body, and then, contrary to the dicta of Locke and Reid, come into being anew with w as his body? Were there, during the day, two persons, x and y, whose bodies were z and w, respectively, and then at some moment during the twilight hours, did x actually come to be identical with this other thing?[9]

I cannot believe that Shoemaker means us to take his suggestion in this literal manner. How, then, are we to take it? I believe that this is the proper interpretation: Since each member of the tribe adopts, toward the nocturnal welfare of a person other than himself, the kind of concern that you and I adopt only toward ourselves, he may find it agreeable or convenient to refer to that other person, when discussing that person's nocturnal affairs, with the kind of linguistic idiom that you and I adopt when we intend to refer only to ourselves. And if these strange people talk in this way, then we may say that, according to *their* concept of a person, it makes perfectly good sense to say that each person "changes his identity" in the evening. But if this is all there is

---

[9]I question, of course, whether it makes any sense to say that there were two persons x and y and that x then came to be identical with the other person y.

to it, can't we say simply that they find it agreeable and convenient, on occasion, to say of different persons that they are really the same? If the people are not deluded, as they were under interpretation (A) above, then they are simply pretending.[10]

V

It should at least be clear from all of this that Shoemaker's approach to these difficult questions is somewhat different from mine. He is right in saying at the end of his paper that, according to my view, the relationship between personal identity and the various criteria he refers to is "a synthetic one." He finds it difficult to understand why, on a view such as mine, "it should be true at all that one should be concerned about one's future welfare when, as must be possible on that view, the future delights and sufferings are not linked to one's 'present self' by our present criteria of personal identity." I agree that there is this possibility on my view. My answer to the question that Shoemaker quotes from Leibniz would be this: Since I *am* concerned about my future welfare, about the welfare of that x such that x is identical with me, and presumably will continue to have this concern, it will follow that, if I should learn that x will some day become King of China, then, even though I also learn that x will then forget everything that x had previously been, I will be as much concerned about the life that x enjoys while King of China as I am about my own; for, given our suppositions, x's welfare will be my own.

Where Mr. Shoemaker is inclined to side with Leibniz, I am

[10]Suppose there were a monarchy in which the subjects found it distasteful ever to affirm that the monarch vacated his throne. Instead of saying that there have been so many dozen kings and queens in the history of their country, they will say that the monarch has now existed for many hundreds of years and has had so many dozen different names. At certain times it has been appropriate that these names be masculine, like "George" and "Henry," and at other times it has been appropriate that they be feminine, like "Victoria" and "Elizabeth." What, then, if we knew about these people and were to hear such talk as this: "There has existed for many hundreds of years an x such that x is our Monarch; x is now feminine, though fifty years ago x was masculine, and fifty years before that x was feminine"? We should not conclude that there was in that land a monarch who is vastly different from any of the people in ours. We should conclude rather that the speaker is either deluded or pretending.

inclined to side with the following observation of Bayle's: "The same atoms which compose water, are in ice, in vapours, in clouds, in hail and snow; those which compose wheat, are in the meal, in the bread, the blood, the flesh, the bones &c. Were they unhappy under the figure or form of water, and under that of ice, it would be the same numerical substance that would be unhappy in those two conditions; and consequently all the calamities which are to be dreaded, under the form of meal, concern the atoms which form corn; and nothing ought to concern itself so much about the state or lot of the meal, as the atoms which form the wheat, though they are not to suffer those calamities, under the form of wheat."[11]

[11]Pierre Bayle, article "Lucretius," Note Q, *A General Dictionary, Historical and Critical,* trans. Rev. J. P. Bernard, Rev. Thomas Birch, John Lockeman, *et al.* (10 vols.; London, 1734–41).

On the Logic of Perception

JAAKKO HINTIKKA

I

The logic of perception as a branch of modal logic. Should the title of this paper prompt you to ask, "What *is* the logic of perception?," there is an answer at hand. I shall argue here that the logic of our perceptual terms is a branch of *modal logic.*[1] In saying this, I mean by "perceptual terms" both such words as "sees," "hears," "feels," etc., which involve a reference to one particular sense modality, and such words as "perceives," which are neutral in this respect. By modal logic, I do not mean only the logic of the terms "necessary" and "possible" but also the logic of all the other terms that can be studied in the same ways as they. Among these terms are most of the words that are usually said to express propositional attitudes, including "knows," "believes," "remembers," "hopes," "strives," etc. What is in common to all the modal notions in this extended sense of the term will be partly explained later.[2]

[1]Mere formalization of the logical behavior of perceptual terms as a branch of modal logic is not by itself very important or interesting. What makes it promising is the existence of a well-developed semantical theory of modal logic. This is due largely to Saul Kripke and Stig Kanger; see Stig Kanger, *Provability in Logic,* Stockholm Studies in Philosophy, vol. I, (Stockholm, 1957); Saul A. Kripke, "Semantical Considerations on Modal Logic," *Acta Philosophica Fennica,* 16 (1963), 83–94; Saul A. Kripke, "Semantical Analysis of Modal Logic I," *Zeitschrift für mathematische Logik und Grundlagen der Mathematik,* 9 (1963), 67–96; Saul A. Kripke, "Semantical Analysis of Modal Logic II," in *The Theory of Models,* Proceedings of the 1963 International Symposium in Berkeley, ed. J. W. Addison, L. Henkin, and A. Tarski (Amsterdam, 1966). Cf. also my papers "Modality and Quantification," *Theoria,* 27 (1961), 119–28, and "The Modes of Modality," *Acta Philosophica Fennica,* 16 (1963), 65–81.

[2]See section II. The characteristic behavior which is explained there in semiformal terms is precisely what the semantical theory of modal logic mentioned in the preceding footnote strives to systematize.

The close relation between theory of perception and modal logic will be argued on two levels. First, I want to outline the basic reasons why the logic of perception is susceptible to the same sort of treatment as other modal logics. Secondly, I want to show, by discussing a number of interrelated problems, that by treating perceptual concepts as modal notions we can shed sharp new light on some of the classical issues in the philosophy of perception. These include the evaluation of the so-called argument from illusion, the status of sense data, and the nature of the objects of (immediate) perception. If I am right, there are interesting connections between these problems and some of the questions we are led to ask when we study the semantics of modal logic in general. Personally, I came to appreciate for the first time the theoretical interest of some of the traditional philosophical problems concerning perception when I realized that they are in effect identical with or at least very closely related to the difficulties logicians and philosophers of logic have recently encountered in trying to understand the interplay between modal notions and the basic logical concepts of identity and existence (of quantification). Problems drawn from the field of perception can even serve to illustrate and to elucidate these general logical and semantical difficulties.

Some of the formal similarities between perceptual terms and other modal terms are obvious enough, so obvious in fact that I find it surprising and perplexing that they should have been registered, to the best of my knowledge, only once in the relevant philosophical literature. In her Howison Lecture, "The Intentionality of Perception: A Grammatical Feature," Miss G. E. M. Anscombe points out a number of similarities between perceptual concepts and concepts she calls intentional.[3] Most of these similarities hold between perceptual notions and modal notions in general. An interesting example is the distinction which Miss Anscombe calls the difference between material and intentional objects (of an activity). A man aims his rifle and fires at a dark patch against the foliage which he takes to be a stag (intentional object). Unknown to him, and most unfortunately, the dark patch was his father (material object), a fact which causes a tragedy. This

[3] Delivered at the University of California, Berkeley, in 1963, and published in *Analytical Philosophy*, ed. R. J. Butler (2d. series; Oxford, 1965), pp. 158–80.

tragedy brings out the importance of the difference between the intentional object aimed at and the material object aimed at. The same distinction clearly applies to perception. Miss Anscombe connects it with Austin's contrast between "Today I saw a man shaved in Oxford," and "Today I saw a man born in Jerusalem," both uttered in Oxford.

The description and perhaps also the formalization of such features of the logic of perception is an interesting and worthwhile enterprise. I do not believe, however, that it can be really successful until we have deeper insights into the way modal notions function and into the reasons why perceptual terms are in this respect like other modal terms.

Modal notions, including propositional attitudes, can be classified according to the degree (kind) of success they presuppose. For instance,

  a knows that *p*

cannot be true unless it is the case that *p*, while, e.g.,

  a believes that *p*
  a hopes that *p*

can both be true even though it is not true that *p*.

The question of the status of perceptual verbs vis-à-vis this distinction is not quite clear, and requires a word of warning. As Gilbert Ryle points out in *The Concept of Mind*,[4] the words "perceive" and "perception" as well as "see," "hear," etc., are normally used "to record observational success." Most of the discussion in this paper is neutral with respect to this distinction, however. A success presupposition is to be read into my use of perceptual terms only when an explicit statement is made to this effect. (In fact, I want to suggest that the interest of the success presupposition and of the correlative possibility of perceptual mistakes is often overrated.) Thus it might be more natural to use locutions like "it appears to *a* that *p*" rather than "*a* perceives that *p*." This would also serve to bring out more clearly what I want to focus on in this paper: the problems connected with one's description of one's immediate perceptual experience (no matter whether it is veridical, unwittingly misleading, or an acknowledged illusion). However, for simplicity, I shall normally employ the shorter locution "perceives that."[5]

---

[4]Gilbert Ryle, *The Concept of Mind* (London, 1949), pp. 222–23.
[5]Another natural possibility would be to follow my commentator's ter-

II

Modal logic as turning on the notion of "possible world." It seems to me that the best way of achieving conceptual clarity in modal logic is to view all the use of modal notions as involving a reference, usually of course only a tacit one, to more than one possible state of affairs or course of events (in short, to more than one "possible world"). In this way, most of the conceptual problems that philosophers of logic have run into in this area become manageable.[6] There is basically nothing unusual or strange in the relation of our terms to their references in modal contexts, I suggest. What seems to cause problems is merely the fact that in such contexts a term may have a reference in more than one "possible world," i.e., that we have to consider our individuals as (potential) members of more than one state of affairs or course of events. Modal contexts thus do not exhibit any *failure of referentiality,* but only *referential multiplicity.* From this point of view, the logic of perception can also be elucidated.

This procedure will be made clearer by my subsequent remarks. There are a few possible misunderstandings, however, against which I first must guard myself. First of all, there is nothing mysterious about what I have called "possible worlds." Following Richard Jeffrey,[7] we might call a "complete novel" a set of sentences in some given language which is consistent but which cannot be enlarged without making it inconsistent. A possible world is precisely what such a complete novel describes. Actually, many useful purposes are served by descriptions of possible worlds that are less than complete, as long as these partial descriptions are large enough to show that the world they purport to describe is really possible. Such partial descriptions of possible

---

minology and speak of "perceptual belief" and "perceptual knowledge." The former is then what my "perceives that" locution is in the first place supposed to cover. I am not quite sure, however, that this terminology is free from misleading connotations.

[6]These problems have been emphasized most persuasively by W. V. Quine; see the relevant parts of his *From a Logical Point of View* (Cambridge, Mass., 1953); *Word and Object* (Cambridge, Mass., 1960); and *The Ways of Paradox* (New York, 1966).

[7]Richard C. Jeffrey, *The Logic of Decision* (New York, 1965), pp. 196–97.

worlds I have called "model sets," and I have discussed them in some detail elsewhere.[8]

Second, it is important to make a distinction between two different cases here. Sometimes (e.g., in the case of the concepts of possibility and necessity) what I have called "possible worlds" are normally different possible *courses of events*. Sometimes (e.g., in the case of perceptual concepts) the relevant "possible worlds" are normally different possible *states of affairs* at the particular moment of time we are talking about. This distinction does not affect what I shall say is the sequel, however.

Third, I am of course not suggesting that the ordinary people who daily use such ordinary words as "sees" or "hears" or "possible" or "necessarily" are ever interested in anything as fancy as "possible worlds" or "possible states of affairs." Surely what they are interested in is just the unique world of ours that happens to be actualized. The point is, rather, that many of the things we all say daily about this actual world of ours can be explicated by a logician in terms of his "possible worlds." A logician might say that we often succeed in saying something about the actual world only by locating it, as it were, on the map of all the different possible worlds.

This is by no means restricted to modal concepts. If I understand a prediction, I know which future courses of events are such that the prediction can be said to have been successful under them, and which courses of events are such that the prediction will have to be said to have failed under them. If I know that the prediction is true, I know that the course which events will actually take ("the actual world") is of the first kind and not of the second. In general, understanding a sentence is being able to divide all possible worlds into two classes: those in which the sentence would be true, and those in which it would be false. For certain technical purposes, the sentence (or the proposition it expresses) might even be identified with the former set of possible worlds. The reason why this gambit succeeds so often should be clear: One understands what a sentence says in so far as one knows what to expect of the world in case the sentence is true.

What is peculiar about modal concepts is only the fact that in

[8]See "Form and Content in Quantification Theory," *Acta Philosophica Fennica,* 8 (1955), 7–55, and "Modality and Quantification."

order to spell out their logic we have to consider several possible worlds in their relation to each other, and not just one possible world at a time, as we can do in explaining the semantics of ordinary, nonmodal logic. The intuitive reason for this difference is that in order to explain what it means for a nonmodal statement to be true in a possible world it suffices to consider that world only, whereas the truth conditions of a modal statement cannot be spelled out without considering possible worlds other than the one in which it is supposed to be true. For instance, "possibly p" can be true in the actual world only if p were true in some (suitable) possible worlds. In other respects, almost the same things could be said of modal sentences as were said above of nonmodal sentences. I know what someone believes if and only if I can tell those possible worlds which are compatible with everything he believes from those which are incompatible with his beliefs. I know what somebody sees at a given moment of time in so far as I can distinguish between states of affairs (at that moment of time) which are compatible with what he sees and states of affairs which are incompatible with his visual perceptions at the time. One can virtually paraphrase all attributions of such "propositional attitudes" as knowledge, belief, wish, hope, perception, etc. to someone in terms of possible worlds compatible with his attitudes at a given moment of time. For instance, we may tentatively put:

(1) a believes that p = in all possible worlds compatible with what a believes it is the case that p;

(2) a does not believe that p (understood in the sense "it is not the case that a believes that p") = there is a possible world compatible with what a believes in which not-p would be true;

(3) a perceives that p = in all possible states of affairs compatible with what a perceives it is the case that p;

(4) a does not perceive that p (understood in the sense "it is not the case that a perceives that p") = there is a possible state of affairs compatible with everything a perceives in which not-p is true.

If it is objected that these equations are but so many tautologies, my answer would be that they are intended to be just that. Their right-hand sides were intended to be merely paraphrases that do not add anything to the expressions on the left-hand side but are in a form somewhat more conducive to conceptual clarity than the original formulation.[9]

One may object that such paraphrases as (1) have the paradoxical consequence that anybody who believes (knows, remembers, etc.) that p believes (knows, remembers, etc.) all the logical consequences of p. This objection is easily parried, however, by understanding "q is compatible with what a believes" as meaning "q is not an analytic consequence of p," where p is a formulation of what a believes and where the notion of analytic consequence is to be understood in one of the senses explained in my paper "Are Logical Truths Tautologies?"[10]

Although such paraphrases as (1) – (4) are thus somewhat crude, they bring out several relevant features of the conceptual situation. From them we can see that whenever we are discussing, say, the beliefs of a given person, the possible worlds we have to consider are the possible worlds compatible with his beliefs. In general, whenever we ascribe or deny a given propositional attitude to a person (with respect to any propositions whatsoever), the possible worlds we have to consider are those compatible with the relevant propositional attitudes of his.[11]

From these paraphrases we can also see in greater detail what forces us to consider several possible worlds in one and the same

---

[9]These paraphrases are not quite accurate, however. They omit the "fine structure" among the different possible worlds, which is due to the fact that not all possible worlds are legitimate "alternatives" to a given one. For the significance and uses of this alternativeness relation, see my works "The Modes of Modality"; *Knowledge and Belief* (Ithaca, N.Y., 1962); and "Quantifiers in Deontic Logic," *Societas Scientiarum Fennica, Commentationes Humanarum Litterarum*, Vol. 23, no. 4 (1957). Incidentally, most of the peculiarities of my somewhat loose use of quotes have undoubtedly caught the reader's eye. For stylistic ease, I am *inter alia* pretending that the letters *"a"* and *"b"* *are* (particular) names or other free singular terms instead of *doing duty for* (arbitrary) names; and likewise for propositional "variables." Furthermore, quotes are omitted from displayed sentences.

[10]See "Are Logical Truths Tautologies?" and "Kant Vindicated," in *Deskription, Analytizität und Existenz*, 3–4 Forschungsgespräch des internationalen Forschungszentrums Salzburg, ed. Paul Weingartner (Pustet, München, and Salzburg, 1966), pp. 215–33 and 234–53, respectively.

[11]In an explicit semantical treatment, this is shown by the fact that these are the only "possible worlds" we have to quantify over.

"logical specious present." It is the possibility of disclaiming a propositional attitude, as in (2) and (4) that necessitates this. If it is said that someone, say a, does not believe that q and that he also does not believe that r, this will be tantamount to saying that there is a possible world compatible with everything a believes in which q would be true and that there is also a similar possible world in which r would be true. There is absolutely no reason for supposing that these two possible worlds are identical, and very often it is on the contrary obvious that they are not. For instance, it is perfectly possible that $r = $ not-q; this merely means that a does not have the opinion that q nor the contrary opinion that not-q. Then requiring that the two possible worlds be identical means requiring that there be a possible world compatible with everything a believes in which both q and not-q would be true, which violates the principle of noncontradictoriness. Hence we often have to consider more than one possible world compatible with someone's propositional attitudes. Only in the case of an omniscient a can we restrict our attention to one world only.

We can see perhaps how intricately involved propositional attitudes are conceptually with the notion of a possible world by asking what it means for someone's propositional attitude to be more extensive than another person's similar attitude. When does a know (believe, wish, perceive) more than b? The only reasonable general answer seems to be that a knows more than b if and only if the class of possible worlds compatible with what he knows is smaller than the class of possible worlds compatible with what b knows; and similarly for the other propositional attitudes. This is not a full answer by any means, for it does not tell us yet how the different possible worlds are to be separated from each other and how they are to be weighted in relation to each other. It suffices to show, nevertheless, how important the notion of a possible world is for our understanding of the logic of propositional attitudes.

III

Quantification and identity in modal contexts. This notion is especially useful in clearing the conceptual muddles that have beset recent attempts to understand the interplay of propositional attitudes and other modal notions with such basic logical concepts as the quantifiers (Ex) ("there is at least one individual, call it x, such that") and (x) ("of each individual, call it x, it is true that") and the concept of identity (of individuals) "$=$." The problems that arise in this area are epitomized by the breakdown of the modes of inference known as "substitutivity of identity" and "existential generalization."[12] The former says, somewhat roughly expressed, that whenever an identity of the form "$a = b$" is true, the terms "a" and "b" are interchangeable everywhere *salva veritate*. The latter says that if a statement containing a free singular term, say "$F(a)$," is true, then so is the result "$(Ex)F(x)$" of replacing this free singular term by a variable bound to an existential quantifier. The striking thing about these two modes of inference is that they seem to be obviously and undoubtedly valid in so far as the only task of our singular terms is merely to refer to the individuals we are talking about. For, if this is the case, how could these two modes of inference go wrong? If two individuals are identical, must not exactly the same things be true of them both? If something is true of the particular individual specified by the term "a," must not this something be true of some individual or other?

Yet these two modes of inference break down in modal contexts. George IV knew that Walter Scott was Walter Scott. Furthermore, Walter Scott was the author of *Waverley*. Nevertheless, the good king did not know that he was, although this would follow by the substitutivity of identity.[13] I may hope that the next governor of California is a Democrat, but it does not follow from this that there is some particular Democrat whom I hope to see elected, contrary to what existential generalization would suggest that I do.

Different philosophers have reacted to this predicament differently. Some have taken the breakdown of these inferences, together with certain further observations, to show that the values of bound variables in modal contexts are something different from

[12]The importance of the breakdown of these two rules of inference has been aptly emphasized by Quine in the works referred to above.

[13]This results by replacing one of the two occurrences of "Walter Scott" in "George IV knows that Walter Scott = Walter Scott" by "the author of *Waverly*" while the other occurrence remains intact. Such partial replacements may seem queer, but are in fact vital in many other, unproblematic contexts.

the ordinary "extensional" entities they usually range over. They have declared that if all these variables did was simply to range over such entities, existential generalization would have to be applicable in these contexts. Others, wary of any unusual "intensional entities," have wanted to explain away those uses of modal concepts which cause the breakdown of the problematic inferences. A frequent device of these philosophers has been the postulation of different senses of propositional attitudes.[14] Some of these senses are allegedly free of the difficulties we have been discussing. A few philosophers have gone so far as to suggest that these "extensional" or "transparent" senses of modal concepts are all that there is to the use of quantification in modal contexts. From the point of view here adopted, this amounts to an attempt to deal with modal concepts as if they could be reduced to concepts that involve a reference to the actual world only, and not to any alternatives to it.

Not many words are needed, however, to restore our confidence in logic without postulating either intensional entities or irreducibly different senses of propositional attitudes. It suffices to recall that each modal notion involves a tacit reference to more than one possible world. The actual truth of the identity "$a = b$" means that the terms "a" and "b" refer to the same individual in the actual world. From this it follows that they are interchangeable in so far as we are speaking of the actual world only, that is to say, in so far as they occur outside the scope of all modal terms. But since modal terms introduce more than one possible world and since there are no general reasons why two terms (like "a" and "b") that actually refer to one and the same individual should do so in other possible worlds, there is not the slightest excuse to think that they are interchangeable in modal contexts.

This is just what is illustrated by our example. The reason why "Walter Scott" and "the author of *Waverley*" were not interchangeable, although they refer to the same person, was that the good king did not know that their references are identical, i.e., that in one of the possible worlds compatible with everything George IV knew, Walter Scott was not the author of *Waverley*.

Similarly, the reason we cannot always generalize existentially

[14]Cf., e.g., W. V. Quine, "Quantifiers and Propositional Attitudes," *Journal of Philosophy*, 53 (1956), 177–87; reprinted in *The Ways of Paradox*.

with respect to a free singular term in a true sentence like "$F(a)$" is that the term in question (our "a") may refer to different individuals in the possible worlds that are brought to play by the modal notions that occur in "$F(a)$." If it refers to different individuals in this way, there is no one individual of whom (or which) we are speaking in saying that $F(a)$, and therefore there is no foothold for maintaining that there is some *individual* (say x) who is such that $F(x)$. This is again exactly what happened in my example: Under the different courses of events compatible with my present hopes, different men will be elected, that is to say, the term "the next governor of California" refers to different individuals in the different "possible worlds" compatible with what I hope to happen. Hence it is not amenable to existential generalization.

Thus the breakdown of existential generalization and of the substitutivity of identity in modal contexts is not a symptom that our free singular terms refer to entities different in kind from their normal references. Rather, the breakdown is a direct consequence of the fact that in modal contexts we have to consider our individuals as members of more than one state of affairs or course of events.

We can also see at once how the problematic inferences are to be restored by means of supplementary premises. In order for the terms "a" and "b" to be interchangeable, they have to refer to the same individual not just in the actual world but also in all the other "worlds" we are considering. For instance, if we are speaking of what d believes, these additional worlds are those compatible with everything he believes. The substitutivity of "a" and "b" thus requires more than the truth of "$a = b$"; it also requires the truth of "d believes that $(a = b)$." Other modalities behave likewise.

To restore existential generalization, we have to assume that the term with respect to which we are generalizing, say "a," refers to the same individual in all the different "worlds" we are considering. They are the actual world plus whatever possible worlds are compatible with the relevant propositional attitudes of the person we are talking about (these do not always include the actual world). The requirement that this should be the case can again be expressed by an explicit premise. In the case of belief it will be

(5) $(Ex)(d$ believes that $(a = x)$ and $(a = x))$

where d is the man we are talking about. The first conjunct in (5) makes sure that the term "a" refers to one and the same individual in all the possible worlds compatible with what d believes, and the second conjunct guarantees that this uniqueness of the reference of "a" extends to the actual world. Analogously, existential generalization is reinstated in perceptual contexts by premises of the form

(6) $(Ex)(d$ perceives that $(a = x)$ and $(a = x))$

where instead of the word "perceives" we could also have one of the more specific words like "sees." Occasionally (for instance, when the veracity of d's perceptions is not at issue, directly or indirectly) we can use instead of (6) the simpler premise

(7) $(Ex)(d$ perceives that $a = x)$.

This premise can be used instead of (6) also if it is required that perceptual terms have a success grammar, that is to say, if it is required that one can perceive only what is in fact the case.

Expressions of form (7) or (6) are extremely interesting in the logic of perception, as their analogues are in other branches of modal logic. Since the effect of (6) is to guarantee that the free singular term "a" refers to one and the same individual in all the possible states of affairs we have to consider, its import may be expressed somewhat inaccurately but nevertheless strikingly by saying that what (6) says is that a is a genuine (unique) individual in so far as d's perceptions are concerned. This way of bringing out the import of expressions like (6) is perhaps even more natural in the case of some of the other modalities. As far as my hopes are concerned, the next governor of California is a (unique) *individual* if and only if there is some one politician who I hope will be elected. As far as your knowledge is concerned, the prime minister of Norway is a unique individual if and only if there is someone who you know is the Norwegian prime minister, in short, in so far as you know who the prime minister of Norway is.

Statements of the form (5) through (7) might also be called "identification statements" (in one possible sense of this expression). There is a sense which one has identified the reference of a term, say "a," if and only if one knows which individual "a" refers to. Likewise, d can be said to have perceptually identified a in so far as he perceives which individual a is, that is to say, in so far as (7) is true. In the case of belief, the simpler identification statement "$(Ex)(d$ believes that $a = x)$" says that d thinks (believes) that he has identified a while the fuller identification statement (5) says in addition that he is in fact right in his belief about the identity of a.

These observations should make it clear that in our treatment of quantification into modal contexts we are not relying on any unusual sense of quantifiers, e.g., a sense to be defined in terms of the truth of substitution-instances of quantified sentences, as some philosophers have tried to do. For instance, the existential quantifier "(Ex)" is here taken to express precisely the *existence* of a (genuine, i.e., unique) *individual*. It is precisely our insistence on this (normal) sense of quantifiers that necessitates the use of additional premises which serve to guarantee that the free singular terms with respect to which we want to quantify really specify unique individuals capable of serving as values of bound individual variables.[15]

This is also what enables us to spell out a part of Miss Anscombe's distinction between the intentional and the material objects of perception. When a free singular term occurs within the scope of a perceptual term in a sentence, it specifies an intentional object. However, if this singular term is replaced by a variable bound to an initial quantifier, we obtain a statement which is not any more about the intentional object, but about the unique individual which as a matter of fact is being perceived, for those are the entities that bound individual variables range over. If it is the case that the relevant value of this variable is a certain individual b, then this individual may be said to be the material object of perception. A paradigm of this distinction is the difference between "d sees that d's brother is being shaved" and "$(Ex)(x = d$'s brother) and (d sees that x is being shaved))," where the former can only be true if d sees that it is his brother who is being shaved, while the latter may be true even when d does not see that the man whom he sees being shaved is in fact his brother. The distinction at any rate catches some of the things

[15]If this were not the case, i.e., if bound variables did not range over genuine individuals, expressions (5) through (7) could scarcely play the role I have assigned to them. For if they failed to do so, the truth of (5) through (7) could not guarantee the kind of uniqueness of reference which is needed if these expressions are to serve as the extra premises that are to safeguard quantification into the modal contexts in question.

Miss Anscombe apparently wants to say of the difference between intentional and material objects of perception, and of the attitudes philosophers have taken to them. It is readily extended to other examples and to other modalities.

The distinction which is illustrated by our paradigm could be called a distinction between statements about, say, *a*, "whoever he is or may be," and statements about the individual (e.g., person or object) who in fact is *a*. This distinction is closely related to our concept of an individual. Only statements of the second kind can really be said to be *about* definite individuals.

IV

The argument from illusion is illusory. How, then, do these observations shed new light on the traditional problems concerning perception? What, for instance, do they imply concerning the status of so-called sense-data, which many philosophers have postulated as objects of immediate perception?

What are these sense-data supposed to be and why do we have to assume them in addition to the ordinary physical objects? I suspect that entirely different things have been included by different philosophers among sense-data. There is a line of argument, however, that once was pretty generally taken to show the indispensability of sense-data in the theory of perception. It is generally known as the "argument from illusion."[16] It has been put forward in several variants. Disregarding the differences between these variants and the subtleties that prompted these differences, we may say that the argument from illusion consists in inferring the necessity of postulating sense-data from the possibility of illusion or perceptual error. In the case of an erroneous perception, for instance in the case of a perception that shows a red object to be grey, the object of one's (immediate) perception cannot (according to this line of thought) be the physical object in question, precisely because its attributes are different from

[16]For surveys and discussions of this argument, see, e.g., Konrad Marc-Wogau, *Die Theorie von Sinnesdaten,* Uppsala Universitets Arsskrift (Uppsala, 1945); A. J. Ayer, *The Foundations of Empirical Knowledge* (London, 1940); J. L. Austin, *Sense and Sensibilia* (Oxford, 1962); Roderick Firth, "Austin and the Argument from Illusion," *Philosophical Review,* 73 (1964), 372–82; A. J. Ayer, "Has Austin Refuted the Sense-Datum Theory?," *Synthese,* 17 (1967), 117–40.

those of the physical object in question. Yet our perceptions are *about* something—there *is* something grey that I do sense even in the case of the illusion we are envisaging. Hence we must assume the existence of nonphysical objects of immediate perception, at least in the case of an illusion. But since there is no intrinsic difference between illusory and veridical perception, it is argued, their objects have to be similar. In both cases, therefore, the objects of immediate perception must be different from ordinary physical objects. These extraordinary objects of immediate perception are then dubbed sense-data.

Although this sketch of the argument from illusion is so brief as to appear a caricature, it brings out some of the relevant features of this line of thought. Presented in this way it seems to me to be completely devoid of force. The basic mistake, or one of the basic mistakes, lies in the vagueness of contrast between the perceived and the real attributes of an object. On any reasonable view of the matter, be it phenomenalistic or realistic, some distinction has to be made between the experienced (phenomenal) qualities and relations of things and their physical qualities and relations. This distinction is usually completely disregarded in the argument from illusion. Yet it is absolutely fatal to many forms of the argument, as Thomas Reid already saw. He formulated a special case of the argument from illusion as follows: "The table which we see, seems to diminish as we remove farther from it; but the real table, which exists independently of us, suffers no alteration. It was, therefore, nothing but its image which was presented to the mind." His reply is: "Let us now suppose, for a moment, that it is the real table we see: Must not this real table seem to diminish as we remove farther from it? It is demonstrable that it must. How then, can this apparent diminution be an argument that it is not a real table? When that which must happen to the real table . . . does happen to the table we see, it is absurd to conclude from this that it is not the real table we see."[17]

Our insight into the nature of perceptual terms as expressing propositional attitudes enables us to point out other mistaken presuppositions in the "argument." Underlying it is obviously the idea that perception is to be construed as a simple two-term relation between the perceiver and the perceived object. For it was

[17]Thomas Reid, *Essays on the Intellectual Powers of Man,* edited and abridged by A. D. Woozley (London, 1941), p. 145.

inferred from the fact that the entity at the receiving end of this relation has attributes different from those a physical object possesses that this entity cannot be identical with that physical object. If the so-called objects of perception enter into the picture only as members of the different possible states of affairs one is perceptually distinguishing from each other, no simple inference of this kind can be drawn.

This line of criticism is somewhat weakened by the fact that we have, in our ordinary usage, constructions with perceptual terms that do not prima facie fit into my view of these terms as expressing propositional attitudes. We have such locutions as "*x* perceives that *p*" or "*x* sees that *p*" where "*p*" is a placeholder for independent clauses, each of which specifies (is true in) a number of "possible worlds." This might be called the propositional construction or "perceiving that" construction. But we also have locutions like "*x* sees *a*" where "*a*" is a free singular term, e.g., a proper name. The latter type of locution might be called the direct-object construction. It suggests a relationship between the perceiver and the objects of perception different from the one we have envisaged so far. The prevalence of this direct-object construction has probably also discouraged interest in the analogies between perceptual concepts and other modal notions. Part of what I have to do to defend my view of the logical behavior of perceptual terms is therefore to show that direct-object constructions with perceptual terms can be reduced to the "perceiving that" construction.

V

An argument from incomplete perceptual identification. More interesting than any criticism of the argument from illusion is perhaps the observation that a different but closely related argument can be put forward for sense-data. This new argument is from our point of view considerably more intriguing than the original argument, although in its simple forms it is much less persuasive than the usual forms of the argument from illusion. This new argument might be called the "argument from incomplete perceptual identification" rather than the argument from illusion. The situations it applies to are in fact much more commonplace than those considered in the argument from illusion.

Consider, for instance, the following situation: There is a piece of chalk (c) on the table in front of someone (d); d perceives that it is white. We might express this as follows:

(8) d sees that $W(c)$.

Now suppose that c is in fact the smallest object on the table:

(9) $c = s$

where "s"= "the smallest object on the table"; and suppose further than d does not see that c is the smallest object on the table and that he does not see in any other way that the smallest object on the table is white:

(10)   not: d sees that $W(s)$.

It is obvious that situations of this kind are perfectly possible, and in fact quite frequent. It may be argued that the possibility of such situations shows that what we are talking about are not ordinary physical objects like pieces of chalk. For if we were talking about them only, surely the certain identity of c and s as physical objects ought to guarantee that exactly the same things can be said of them, i.e., that the terms "c" and "s" are interchangeable everywhere (*salva veritate*). But this is just what is not the case in the situation we envisaged, for there the substitution of "s" for "c" in (8) turns it into the statement

(11) d sees that $W(s)$,

which contradicts (10). Hence the objects of perception we are talking about here must be something different from ordinary physical objects. They might, for all that I can see, be labeled sense-data.

A closely related argument might run as follows: If what we are talking about in (8) through (10) were ordinary physical objects, we ought to be able to generalize existentially with respect to c in (8) and obtain

(12) (Ex) $(d$ sees that $W(x))$,

where the bound variable x ranges over ordinary physical objects. But it can scarcely do so in (12), for what is the physical object whose existence makes (12) true? It cannot be c, for as a physical object c is identical with s, of which it is not true at all that d sees that it is white. But if it is not c, it is hard to see what this physical object could be. Hence the values of the bound variable x in (12) have to be something different from ordinary physical objects. There does not seem to be anything wrong with calling them sense-data.

VI

Sense-data as intensional entities. It is obvious that this "argument from incomplete perceptual identification" for the existence of sense-data presents us with a situation that is precisely analogous to the predicament into which the breakdown of the substitutivity of identity and of existential generalization put us in ordinary modal logic. The line of thought of those who were willing to posit sense-data on the basis of our argument would be analogous to the line of thought of those philosophers of logic who have been led to resort to intensional entities in understanding quantification into modal contexts. In other respects, too, there seems to be a great deal in common to the theory of perception and to the philosophy of modal logic. For instance, some philosophers apparently want to avoid speaking of what seems to be the case to someone as a primitive or irreducible idea. These locutions they would like to see reduced to expressions in which we only speak of what is. These philosophers are from a logician's point of view so many unwitting allies of those modal logicians who would like to avoid all talk of possible worlds different from the actual one. Whoever suggests that to talk of how things look to us is to talk, not of ourselves, but of certain aspects of these (ordinary physical) things, of their looks,[18] is tacitly sympathizing with those philosophers of modal logic who are willing to countenance only referentially transparent senses of modal notions as being fully legitimate. In short, in the last analysis John Langshaw Austin may have been the Willard Van Quine of perception theory.

In spite of these similarities, the connection between intensional entities and sense-data may still seem somewhat tenuous. It is true that sense-datum theories have taken forms whose originators would disown all connection of their ideas with an argument from incomplete perceptual identification. Nevertheless, there are more similarities between sense-data and intensional entities than we have so far discovered. Pointing out some of them may perhaps reduce an impression of tenuousness.

---

[18]Cf. Austin, *Sense and Sensibilia,* p. 43: "I am not disclosing a fact about *myself,* but about petrol, when I say that petrol looks like water. . . . Is it not that . . . looks and appearance provide us with *facts* on which a judgement may be based . . . ?"

For instance, it may be asked: Should not sense-data be *data* and not individuals (in the logical sense of the word)? Are we not misrepresenting their status by turning them from the facts perceived (apparently perceived) into the ultimate objects (individuals) to which perceived attributes belong?

One answer is that our conception of sense-data (if any) is essentially that of G. E. Moore and of a number of other prominent philosophers, however it may be related to that of less careful and explicit sense-datum theorists. In order to show this, it suffices to quote the way in which Moore introduces sense-data in his lectures on *Some Main Problems of Philosophy* in 1910–11. Moore is considering a certain visual impression of his. "These things: this patch of whitish colour, and its size and shape I did actually see. And I propose to call these things, the colour and size and shape, *sense-data,* things *given* or presented by the senses —given, in this case, by my sense of sight" (Moore's italics).[19] "These things," although intended to be *things,* are perhaps not yet individuals in the logical sense of the word. But Moore soon saw the light. When the lectures were published in 1953, Moore added the following remark to the quoted passage: "I should now make, and have for many years made, a sharp distinction between what I have called the 'patch,' on the one hand, and the colour, size, and shape, *of* which is is, on the other; and should call, and have called, *only* the patch, *not* its colour, size, or shape, a 'sense-datum'." I cannot think of a clearer statement showing that sense-data were for Moore *individuals.*[20]

It may also be questioned whether the sense-data that someone might be inclined to introduce by an argument from incomplete

---

[19]*Some Main Problems of Philosophy* (London, 1953), p. 44. For the importance of this point for the rest of sense-datum philosophy, see *ibid.,* p. 45, n. 6.

[20]The same fact emerges clearly from the pronouncements of several of the other well-known sense-datum theorists. See, e.g., H. H. Price, *Perception* (London, 1932), p. 64: "For we are acquainted with *particular instances* of redness, roundness, hardness and the like, and such *instances of* such *universals* are what one means by the term sense-data" (my italics), or Bertrand Russell, *Mysticism and Logic* (London, 1918), p. 147: "When I speak of a 'sense-datum,' I do not mean the whole of what is given in sense at one time. I mean rather such as part of the whole as might be singled out by attention: *particular* patches of color, *particular* noises, and so on" (my italics).

perceptual identification can serve any of the epistemological purposes which sense-data are traditionally taken to serve (and sometimes specifically introduced to serve). In answering this query, I am somewhat handicapped by the fact that I do not believe that there are sense-data in any usual sense of the word, and hence cannot say what they perhaps might be good for. It is a fact, however, that if the characteristic features of intensional entities, as they are usually conceived of by philosophers, are attributed to sense-data, we find ourselves ascribing to sense-data some of precisely those features that allegedly made sense-data so attractive epistemologically. For instance, Quine says (or used to say) that any two ways of characterizing one and the same intensional entity (in ordinary modal contexts) must be analytically (necessarily) equivalent:[21] "$i = j$" implies "necessarily $(i = j)$" if i and j are intensional entities. The analogue to this would be to say that whenever two sense-data are in fact identical, they are perceived to be identical. It is, in this sense, impossible to make perceptual mistakes about the identity of sense-data. If there were such entities, they would be epistemologically privileged, at least in this sense. It might thus be said that sense-data are at least as respectable, and as difficult to avoid, as intensional entities are in modal logic.

We have already seen, however, that they are a pretty disrespectable bunch of entities. We have already seen that the kinds of argument which I labeled "argument from incomplete perceptual identification" do not suffice to justify the conclusions they purport to justify. The features of the logical behavior of perceptual concepts which apparently needed the postulation of sense-data can be accounted for by observing the character of these concepts as involving a simultaneous reference to several possible states of affairs, along the lines indicated above for modal notions in general. For instance, we can generalize existentially with respect to the term "s" in the example above only if this term refers to one and the same individual in all the possible situations we have to consider here. Since these are all the possible states of affairs compatible with what d perceives, existential generalization is possible if and only if there is some individual x to which "s" refers in all these states of affairs. This means, however, that d

---

[21]See, e.g., Quine, *From a Logical Point of View*, pp. 151–52.

sees that *s* is this individual *x*. Hence the extra premise needed is again of the form

(13) $(Ex)(d$ sees that $(s = x))$.

Thus there does not seem to be any force in the arguments for sense-data we have considered so far. What has been said is not the whole story, however, and what remains to be said puts the matter into a somewhat different perspective.

VII

Individuation as a prerequisite of the use of quantifiers. In the account I have given of the logic of propositional attitudes, I have so far disregarded certain very important presuppositions. I have said, for instance, that a free singular term is amenable to existential generalization if and only if it refers to one and the same individual in all the different "possible worlds" we have to consider in the relevant context. Now this clearly presupposes that it makes sense to say that a member of one of the possible worlds *is the same individual* as a member of another possible world. In short, the account I have given of the logic of propositional attitudes and other modal notions presupposes that we can make what might be called cross-identifications, that is to say, identifications across the boundaries of possible worlds, or identifications between members of different possible worlds.

Since it was the identity of the respective references of a singular term in the different possible worlds we are considering that made it possible to say that it specifies a unique *individual,* the method of cross-identification which is presupposed in my account of the logic of propositional attitudes might also be called a method of *individuation* in contexts governed by propositional attitudes. Since variables bound to quantifiers range over individuals, a method of individuation is an indispensable prerequisite of all quantification into modal contexts. A quantifier that binds (from the outside) a variable occurring in a modal context does not make any sense without such a method of individuation, and its meaning is relative to this method.

At this point, it would be tempting to say simply that since quantification into modal contexts often makes perfectly good sense (even when these contexts are *not* construed transparently), we obviously must have as a part of our normal conceptual structure such methods of individuation. That this is in fact the case is clear enough. But it is nevertheless worth one's while to take a somewhat closer look at the situation.

Consider, for instance, the concept of knowledge. Here the possible worlds we have to heed are described by all the different "complete novels" compatible with what someone knows. It is clear that in most cases a comparison between two such novels will show fairly soon whether an individual figuring in one is identical with an individual described in the other. It is also fairly obvious what sorts of clues we would use in deciding this. They would be essentially the same kinds of leads we in fact use in reidentifying (in Strawson's sense) individuals.[22] What these are in the case of the different kinds of individuals is a difficult philosophical problem. (What constitutes personal identity, for instance?) It is amply clear, however, that for a wide variety of circumstances we have methods of cross-identification or individuation in the required sense, however difficult they are to describe with a full philosophical clarity. Furthermore, it is clear that an attempt to describe these criteria is not the business of a poor modal logician. To describe the criteria of personal identity is part of the business of a philosopher of psychology, and the task of describing the other kinds of the individuation methods belongs to the province of branches of philosophy, maybe partly to the philosophy of biology and of physics. I do not see much reason to worry whether suitable methods of individuation exist, although my philosophical colleagues may find plenty to worry about in the question of exactly how the methods we ordinarily rely on are to be described.

Essentially the same can be said of all the other propositional attitudes. The methods we use to individuate the objects of such attitudes are again essentially like our ordinary methods of re-identifying individuals, and hence relatively unproblematic for a logician.

Even a logician has to observe, however, that these methods

---

[22]Here we have something more than a mere similarity, namely, an analogy. In the one case (reidentification) we are dealing with identifications between members of temporally different states of affairs, in the other (different possible worlds) we normally identify individuals occurring under different possible courses of events. It is clear that some considerations are common to the two cases, although there obviously are also dissimilarities.

of individuation rely heavily on certain contingent (nonconceptual) features of our environment. Without going into any detail, we still can see it is obvious that these methods of individuation turn on such facts as bodily continuity, continuity of memory, certain obvious features of the behavior of material bodies vis-à-vis space and time (one and the same body cannot be at two places at the same time; it takes time for it to get from one place to another; it does not change its shape or size instantaneously, etc.), and many similar physical and psychological regularities. To have a word for these methods of individuation, I shall call them *physical* methods of individuation or cross-identification. There may be good conceptual reasons why the methods of individuation which we ordinarily rely on make use of these regularities, but there does not seem to be any conceptual necessity that they, and only they, should be exploited for the purpose of individuating the objects of the various propositional attitudes. If certain doctrines of reincarnation were taken seriously, and if it really were possible to find out about people's earlier incarnations, our methods of individuation would have to be changed. If the equally improbable motto of the Wykehamists were literally true and manners were what "maketh man," other criteria of individuation than such mundane things as bodily continuity would be needed. Certainly we can imagine a primitive tribe playing one of those Wittgensteinian language games in which the successive kings and medicine men are really one and the same person, irrespective of differences in looks and memories, as the successive Dalai Lamas are believed to be one and the same person by the true believers.

VIII

Perceptual vs. *physical methods of individuation.* The possible multiplicity of methods of individuation is not of great interest, however, so long as it is not exhibited by our own conceptual system. Now the great interest of perceptual concepts for a philosopher of logic is due precisely to the fact that in connection with them we all as a matter of fact use two different methods of individuation. One of them is the method of physical individuation indicated above, but the other is essentially different from it.

It seems to me that a great deal of the logic of perception is connected with this very fact.

What, then, is this other method of individuation? In order to see what it is, let us consider what someone, d, sees at some particular moment of time. Let us assume that he sees a man in front of him but that he does not see who the man is. Here the relevant "possible worlds" are all the different states of affairs at the time in question that are compatible with everything he sees. We have already seen what it means to cross-identify individuals in different possible states of affairs by means of physical methods of individuation. By these methods, the man in front of d (let us call him m) is a different individual (different person) in some of the relevant possible states of affairs: just because d does not see who m is, the individual to whom the term "m" refers will be a different physico-psychological individual (different person) in some of the different states of affairs compatible with everything d sees then and there. In all these different states of affairs, however, there has to be a man in front of d. (Otherwise the state of affairs in question would not be compatible with what d sees.) The common perceptual relation of these different men to d separates them from the other individuals in each of the possible situations we are considering. Because of this, we may say that from the point of view of d's perceptual situation they are after all one and the same man—the man in front of him.

This obviously can be generalized. When presented with descriptions of two different states of affairs compatible with what d sees, and with two individuals figuring in these two respective descriptions, we can ask whether they are identical as far as d's visual impressions are concerned, and often we can answer this question. This question therefore gives us another method of individuating objects in contexts in which we are talking of what someone sees at a given moment of time, and a generalization to other perceptual terms is forthcoming.

We shall call individuals so cross-identified "perceptually individuated" objects. Earlier we encountered "physically individuated" objects. It would be suggestive and in many respects illuminating to call these two "physical objects" and "perceptual objects," respectively. In a way, this is just what is involved. What enabled us to say that the man in front of d is a unique visually individuated individual might be expressed precisely by saying that from *d*'s point of view there is in fact such a visual object as the man in front of him.

Striking though this way of speaking is, it is highly misleading. There is no question here of any ontological difference between different kinds of entities. The individuals which exist in the different possible worlds that we have to consider are of the same kind ontologically as the individuals existing in the actual world. There is no distinction between free singular terms referring to physically individuated objects and those referring to perceptually individuated objects. The only difference lies in the distinction between the two methods of individuation. This is a matter of the relation of the different possible states of affairs to each other. It does not appear as long as we are merely considering the different states of affairs one by one; it becomes relevant only when an implicit or explicit comparison between different states of affairs is made.

IX

Two kinds of quantifiers and their meaning. We have already seen that quantification into a context governed by a perceptual term involves such a comparison. Hence the meaning of quantifiers that from the outside bind variables occurring inside perceptual constructions (e.g., within the scope of the expression "sees that") will depend on the method of individuation employed. In other words, when quantifying into perceptual contexts we have to reckon with two different pairs of quantifiers with different meanings. The variables bound to them range over the same sort of individuals, but differently individuated. We shall reserve the symbols "(Ex)" and "(x)" for quantifiers relying on physical methods of individuation. As quantifiers turning on perceptual methods of individuation, we shall use "$(\exists x)$" and "(Vx)," respectively. Here it would again be tempting to say that variables bound to (Ex) and (x) range over physical objects while those bound to $(\exists x)$ and (Vx) range over perceptual objects. Saying this might even be illuminating for certain limited purposes. However, it will obscure the fact that ours is not simply a case of many-sorted quantification but that the relation between the two pairs of quantifiers is subtler than that. In general, in the kind of situation with which we are dealing, it is not illuminating to speak of quantifiers as *ranging over* a class of individuals. The conceptual situation is too complicated to be adequately described by this locution.

The distinction between different kinds of quantifiers is of considerable interest. One place where the distinction is relevant is a statement of perceptual identification. Since these turn on the use of quantifiers, we now have to distinguish between two sorts of perceptual identification. One of them will be expressed by a statement like

(7) (Ex) $(d$ perceives that $a = x)$,

while the other will be expressed by statements of the form

(14) $(\exists x)$ $(d$ perceives that $b = x)$.

What does the distinction between (7) and (14) amount to intuitively? This can be seen most clearly by considering cases in which (7) and (14) are true but only contingently (nontrivially) true. Cases in point are obtained by making $a =$ the man in front of d and $b =$ Mr. Smith. Then (7) will say that there is some physically individuated person x (individual) with whom a is identical in all the states of affairs compatible with what d perceives. In other words, d perceives that the man in front of him is this particular person (physical object) x. This, clearly, is tantamount to d's *perceiving who* the man in front of him is. More generally, an approximate translation of (7) into a more idiomatic mode of discourse will be

$(7a)$ d perceives what (or who) a is.

This is parallel to the familiar "knowing what" or "knowing who" construction which we have already met.

What, then, about the other kind of identification, typified by (14)? There it is said that one of d's perceptually individuated objects (his "perceptual objects") is perceptually identified by d with Mr. Smith. In other words, d can (so to speak) find a place for Mr. Smith among his perceptual objects; Mr. Smith is one of his perceptual objects; in short, he *perceives Mr. Smith.* More generally, the appropriate translation of (14) into "ordinary language" will be something like

$(14a)$ d perceives b.

The difference between (7) and (14) is thus the same as the difference between d's seeing who the man in front of him is and d's seeing Mr. Smith.

Several comments are in order here. First of all, it is encouraging to see one of the distinctions which we have arrived at on the basis of abstract logical and semantical considerations to be reflected faithfully by perfectly ordinary language. This suggests strongly that we are on the right track here.

In fact, the only reason I have not been more categorical about the relation of our statements (7) and (14) to the vernacular locutions (7a) and (14a) is that these vernacular expressions often involve various existence and success presuppositions. We have all the methods at our disposal for incorporating these presuppositions into our formal statements (7) and (14) by adding suitable supplementary clauses. I shall not investigate here when and how they are to be added.

I should point out, however, that a statement involving a direct-object construction, e.g. (14a), is in ordinary usage sometimes construed as a statement about the individual in question, not about b "whoever he is or may be." According to what was said earlier toward the end of section III, the force of the vernacular direct-object construction (14a) is then more likely to be expressible by

$$(15) \quad (\exists x) \ (x = b \text{ and } d \text{ perceives that } x \text{ exists})$$

than by (14).[23]

Secondly, the translatability of (14) as (14a) or as (15) shows that we have now found an analysis of the direct-object construction in terms of quantifiers and of "perceiving that." The direct-object construction is therefore not an irreducible way of using perceptual terms. We have seen, on the contrary, that in order to spell out its precise meaning and its difference from the "perceiving what (who)" construction we have to analyze carefully the presuppositions of the use of quantifiers in perceptual contexts. The presence of the direct-object construction in our ordinary language therefore does not go to show that objects can, logically speaking, enter into perceptual situations otherwise than as members of the different possible states of affairs we are implicitly considering here. Rather, on my analysis, it reinforces my

---

[23]Our frequent preference of (15) to (14) as a translation of (14a) is brought out by the fact that (14a) is often thought of as being subject to the substitutivity of identity: if d perceives b, he perceives it under any name or description. When this is the case, (15) is a better translation than (14).

point than this is the *only* way in which they enter into the logic of perception, and that there is no way out of the propositional-attitude character of our perceptual concepts.[24]

In terms of the behavior of singular terms vis-à-vis the two sorts of quantifiers, we can now make certain secondary distinctions between different kinds of free singular terms. It was already said above that the difference is *not* due to a difference in the individuals they refer to. There are not any strange entities here to be referred to. There may be differences between different kinds of free singular terms, however, in that the way in which some terms refer to the individuals they in fact refer to depends more on the perceptual situation, while the way other terms refer turns more on physical criteria and on other features independent of the particular perceptual situation we are considering.[25] On the logical level, this difference is betrayed by the fact that former kinds of singular terms are more likely to make (14) true when substituted for "*b*" than the latter, which conversely makes (7) true more often than the former when substituted for "*a*." For some particular substitution values of "*a*" and "*b*", (7) and (14) might even be analytically true (i.e., true for conceptual reasons). In such cases, we might be tempted to extend the distinction between perceptual (perceptually individuated) objects and physical (physically individuated) objects to the referents of free singular terms. More appropriately, we might perhaps speak of physically presented and perceptually presented objects. This would again be misleading, however, for the difference is between different kinds of singular terms, and not at all between their references. Moreover, even the difference between the terms is in evidence only when these terms are allowed to mingle with quantifiers.

With these qualifications in mind, it might nevertheless be illuminating to describe the difference between (7) and (14) as follows: In the former, a perceptually presented object is iden-

---

[24]Cf. Moore's formulation of a closely related point: "We should then have to say that expressions of the form 'I believe so-and-so,' 'I conceive so-and-so,' though they undoubtedly express *some* fact, do *not* express any relation between *me* on the other hand and an object of which the name is in the words we use to say *what* we believe or conceive" (*Some Main Problems of Philosophy,* p. 288).

[25]Demonstratives are typical instances of the former, proper names of the latter.

tified with a physical individual, whereas in the latter a physically presented object is identified with a perceptual individual.

Of course, it is perfectly possible that, unlike the terms we chose to instantiate "*a*" and "*b*" in (7) and (14), the former of these terms might rely predominantly on physical and the latter predominantly on perceptual methods of presentation. The only thing that happens then is that (7) and (14) become trivially true in most cases, and therefore less useful for our illustrative purposes than the statements we have considered.

A partial comparison with Miss Anscombe's paper is perhaps in order here. Our remarks on (14), (14a), and (15) show that the two kinds of constructions discussed in section III (one used in making statements about a definite individual and the other used in making statements about whoever happens to be referred to by a singular term) are found with either of the two kinds of quantifiers. If the former difference is used to explicate Miss Anscombe's distinction between the material and intentional objects of perception, we thus have to say that her distinction cuts across our distinction between quantifiers that rely on physical methods of cross-identification and quantifiers that rely on perceptual methods of cross-identification. I have some difficulty in understanding fully Miss Anscombe's fascinating paper, but even so it seems to be clear that this cannot be the whole story. In many places Miss Anscombe seems to assimilate the distinction between intentional and material objects of perception to some kind of a distinction between perceptual and physical objects, a distinction which presumably has to be explicated in terms of a difference between different kinds of quantifiers or different kinds of occurrences of bound variables.

There need not be anything wrong with Miss Anscombe's distinction nor with my attempted reconstruction of it, apart from understandable vagueness. Miss Anscombe concentrates on the direct-object construction with perceptual terms. In our terms, this means that quantifiers relying on perceptual methods of individuation are being used. In such circumstances, the difference between the two constructions examined in section III becomes largely a distinction between the use of singular terms (including variables bound to perceptual quantifiers) *outside* contexts governed by a perceptual term and *inside* such contexts. Outside such contexts, they merely serve to refer to an ordinary actually existing individual (or range over such individuals). By contrast, inside such a construction a bound variable involves the kind of "perceptually individuated individual" which seems to be closely related to what Miss Anscombe has in mind, and in speaking of intentional objects of perception a free singular term can enter into an identity statement together with such a bound variable and in this sense also involve perceptual individuation. The difference between the roles of *b* in (14) and (15) is a clear case in point. Thus it is not hard to see how someone can easily assimilate to each other the distinctions between different kinds of quantification and different kinds of individuals when discussing the objects of perception. This assimilation obstructs clarity in this area, however, and it is advisable to keep the different distinctions as sharply separate as possible.

X

Sense-data as hypostatizations of perceptual methods of individuation. Perhaps the most interesting perspective opened by our observations is the possibility of appreciating what seem to me to be the deeper motives of the sense-datum talk. I see no reason to retract my earlier suggestion that there are no such members of our world as sense-data. However, we can perhaps now see one way in which they can easily steal their way into one's thinking, and that they have a certain justification. The closest legitimate approximation to sense-data that I can find are the values of those quantifiers that rely on perceptual methods of individuation. If their values could be reified into perceptual objects, these objects would be the legitimate heirs of sense-data. It seems to me justified to think of sense-data as having come about in this very way. Viewed in this light, sense-datum talk represents a dramatization of certain important features in the logical behavior of quantifiers relying on perceptual methods of individuation. The dramatic fiction of this sense-datum talk is a hypostatization of the values of variables bound to such quantifiers into alleged entities different from the ordinary ones.

How fully our quantifiers "$(\exists x)$" and "$(\forall x)$" serve the purposes sense-data were designed to serve is perhaps seen from the fact that their use can be justified by an argument which is but a slight variation of the argument from incomplete perceptual identification. Suppose I see a number of people but that I do not see who they are. Because of this failure, I cannot speak of them as those fully individuated persons (physically individuated individuals) who they (unseen by me, so to speak) in fact are. If I nevertheless want to speak of them as individuals (in the logical sense of the word), I must use other methods of individuation. This, in a nutshell, is the reason that perceptual methods of individuation are needed; and, recalling the argument from incomplete perceptual identification, it scarcely seems too far-fetched to say that it is also the true gist of this argument.

Thus viewed, sense-datum theories have the merit of a vigorous attempt to call our attention to certain interesting features of our conceptual system. They constitute a splendid example of revisionary metaphysics, incidentally illustrating most of the weaknesses of metaphysics sans logic. They anticipate perfectly valid logical distinctions, but exaggerate them beyond recognition. It might appear plausible to say that wherever there are different methods of individuation, there are also individuals of essentially different kinds, but this simply is not the case.

Although I thus find myself denying that the logical distinction between the two kinds of quantifiers has any ontological significance, I have a suspicion that a little more is at stake here than a pure logician is interested in. I suspect the kind of logical distinction I have made is exactly what those philosophers have had dimly in mind who have put forward and tried to defend such ontological distinctions as, for example, those between sense-data and physical objects. At any rate, if my suspicions are justified, we have reached a nice extension of Quine's dictum. Quine said that to be is to be a value of a bound variable. I suspect that to be in ontologically different senses is but to be a value of different kinds of bound variables.

XI

The element of truth in sense-datum theories. So far, I have emphasized that there are no sense-data in any ontologically relevant sense of the term. No individuals in any possible world are likely to include any such entities; they exist neither here nor there as far as ordinary existence as an "inhabitant" of a possible world is concerned.

The other side of the coin is that methods of cross-identification inevitably create an objectively delineated supply of ways of individuating an object or person (in the context of some given propositional attitude of some definite person). They can be envisaged as functions (or partial functions) which from each possible world under consideration pick out (at most) one individual, *the same in all these worlds.* They are thus correlated one-to-one with the "genuine" individuals we can speak of in the relevant context, and are therefore perhaps the closest counterpart to our intuitive idea of individual that we can incorporate in an explicit semantical theory.

In the case of d's beliefs, each of these functions is correlated with some singular term *"a"* such that (Ex) [d believes that $(a = x)$ and $(a = x)$] is true.

In spelling out the semantics of quantification into contexts governed by words for propositional attitudes we have to quantify over these functions (different ways of specifying a unique individual). In the case of quantifiers relying on perceptual methods of individuation, they will share some of the characteristics of the alleged sense-data. If they are what sense-data were intended to be, then there exist such things as sense-data.

This seems to be too hasty a conclusion, however. It is true that by Quine's criterion they would seem to be part of our ontology, since we have to quantify over them. This impression is misleading, however, and in fact brings out a clear-cut and important failure of Quine's dictum, construed as a criterion of *ontological* commitment. The functions in question are not inhabitants of any possible world; they are not part of the furniture of our actual world or of any (other) possible world. Thus it would be extremely misleading to count them in in any census of one's ontology. What they represent is, rather, an objectively given supply of ways in which *we* can deal with more than one contingency (possible world). They are part of our conceptual repertoire or our *ideology* (in something like Quine's sense) rather than a part of our *ontology*. In a sense, we are committed to their *existence,* in the sense of their objectivity, but not to including them among *"what there is"* in the actual world or in any other world.

After a somewhat tortuous discussion, we have thus found a sense in which something like sense-data do exist. Yet it is only fair to say that we have also found that all the usual sense-datum theories are clearly wrong. They involve the fallacious hypostatization mentioned above and which we can now describe as an attempt to roll together the different values of these functions (which pick out individuals from different possible worlds) and reify them into something like ordinary individuals (of which one could ask such questions as what their relation to material bodies is).

For propositional attitudes other than perceptions, there exist by the same token "intensional objects," however different those function-like entities are from ordinary bona fide individuals. A glimpse of the relation of these intensional entities to some traditional distinctions can perhaps be obtained from a quick comparison with Frege's formulations. His idea of the *sense* (*Sinn*) of a singular term, Frege avers, contains more than the idea of *reference* (*Bedeutung*), because in it we also have to include *the way in which the reference is given to us* (*die Art des Gegebenseins*).[26] Our intensional entities (remember that they are functions, not individuals) can be said to include not the way their references are given to us, but *the way in which they are* (*or can be*) *individuated*. From our point of view, an intensional entity—if the term is at all apt here, which I am rather dubious about—is a particular way of individuating an object, of specifying a unique, well-defined individual. They are objectively determined to the extent the truth values of statements containing such locutions as "knows who," "perceives who," "has an opinion concerning the identity of," "perceives (plus a direct object)," etc. are objectively determined.

This comparison with Frege also illustrates our disagreement with him. Any old way of picking out some individual or other from each possible world can be said to be a way of giving us an individual, but only if the individual is the same one in all the relevant possible worlds can it be said to amount to a way of *individuating* an object (or person).

The full import of these brief remarks can only be spelled out by describing in greater detail the semantics of perceptional terms and of other propositional attitudes. For reasons of space, it can-

[26]Gottlob Frege, "Sinn und Bedeutung," *Zeitschrift für Philosophische Kritik*, N.S., 100 (1892), 25–50, esp. 26–27.

not be done here. Nor can the similarities and contrasts between perception and other propositional attitudes be examined in any further detail.

Suffice it to say merely that we can provide a partial answer to a question that no doubt has bothered you ever since we started comparing sense-data with intensional entities. If the arguments for both of them are parallel, why is there so much more of a palpable temptation to postulate sense-data than to postulate any shadowy intensional entities? The obvious answer is that in the case of many other propositional attitudes there is nothing corresponding to perceptual methods of individuation. Since our approximations toward sense-data turned on a contrast between these methods and the ordinary physical methods of cross-identification, in the case of other propositional attitudes we do not have the same temptation to assume nonphysical entities as in the case of perception.

Some other propositional attitudes nevertheless allow methods of individuation that turn on the personal situation (or past situations) of the person in question rather than on physical criteria of cross-identification. Although I cannot here discuss them as fully as they deserve, it seems to me that for these other propositional attitudes, too, personal methods of individuation go together with the ubiquitous direct-object construction. Memory and to some extent knowledge are cases in point.

Comments

ROMANE CLARK

Professor Hintikka's recent work seems to me so philosophically important, and his present paper so ingenious and nearly right, that it is with some relief that I find an area of disagreement which is not just nit-picking. If I am correct, the disagreement has the merit of making a difference in what one believes about the nature of perception and not just the nature of modal logic. To develop the differences between my understanding of what he says and what I believe to be the truth, I shall need to back up a bit.

Hintikka's central claim is that the logic of perception is a modal logic. Although his claim, I think, is correct, it is more radical than it may seem. One consequence of his claim is that sense-data emerge as intensional entities. The claim has then some philosophical point. He justifies the claim by suggesting how the semantics of modal logic, and the model sets of *Knowledge and Belief* (Ithaca, N.Y., 1962) can be used to make clear certain concepts of perception. The claim is plausible since perceptual assertions are heir to the same failures of existential generalization and substitutivity of identities as are assertions of necessity or of belief. Moreover, these inferential principles can be reconstituted for perceptual assertions in a manner similar to the way they can be reconstituted for assertions of necessity and belief. These inferential failures, and Hintikka's reconstitutions of the principles of inference, are instructive in going on to assess the detail of his treatment of perceptual assertions. We shall turn immediately to his account of the failure of these familiar principles of logical inference, pausing only briefly to emphasize how very bold, and so how very interesting, Hintikka's claim is.

It is not at all obvious that the logic of perception is a species of the logic of belief. It is not at all obvious that the logic of belief is a modal logic. The latter is not obvious because the concept of belief is a categorematic one and essentially involves reference to persons and the occasions upon which they think what they do. Assertions of necessity, by contrast, need not involve any such references and the concept of necessity is a logical, syncategorematic, concept. It is the great virtue of Hintikka's earlier work that he has shown that this difference, and other, subtler ones, are superficial, that the semantics of belief is a variant of the semantics of necessity and possibility.

It is not obvious either that the logic of perception is a species of the logic of belief. But it is, I think, true that it is. It is the considerable merit of Hintikka to suggest how, despite commonsense differences in the concepts of the two areas, this is to be understood. The gross differences between assertions of belief and assertions of perceptual knowledge that immediately strike one tend to fall into types. There are those that turn on the fact that perspective is essentially involved in what we perceive but not in what we believe. (You stand, blocking my view. You prevent me from seeing, but not from believing, what is the case.) There are those that turn on the sensuous immediacy of experience, tying the act to the occasion, by contrast with the free range of thought and belief. (I believe what is false, or think of one who is absent. But I do not perceive what is false, or detect one who is absent. Again, I see something, I know not what, and suspend judgment about it. But I do not believe, or think of, something, I know not what, and suspend judgment about it.) Some differences turn on the objects of perception and of belief. (To think of John is perhaps always to think something about John. But it is not clear that to detect a trace in the air is to perceive something about it. Or, I hear an unidentified sound, you hear the squeak of brakes in the drive, and she hears that her teen-aged son is returning from his midnight pleasures.) These gross, and apparent, differences—and presumably other, more subtle, ones—turn out, given Hintikka's account, to be relatively superficial or only apparent differences. To perspective and occasion, there is the contrast between physical and perceptual modes of identifying the objects of belief and perception, together with the apparatus of matching quantifiers. These objects are the same objects, though the modes of their individuation or identification are strikingly different. To the direct objects of experience, there is Hintikka's reduction of direct-object constructions to propositional forms. We need to look at some of the detail of the apparatus and the reduction. Since that begins with the failure of the inferential principles and the manner of their reconstitution, we start with these.

It is pretty clear in ascribing beliefs or perceptions to agents that there is a familiar but fundamental contrast between the objects and beliefs of those of us who are scribes, recording the event, and the beliefs or perceptions we record and ascribe to an agent. We say that the agent knows or sees such-and-such and commit *ourselves* thereby to the truth of such-and-such. Scribe may say that Agent believes when Agent, giving voice to his beliefs, would say he knows. Scribe knows perhaps that what the agent believes isn't so. The logical principles of existential generalization and the substitutivity of identity reflect the dual subjectivity of these ascriptions, though with a slight and interesting difference.

(I digress to remark that there is a large and interesting difference between the cases that concern us now and the case in which we generalize existentially from assertions recording the occurrence of sensations: the baby hears and is startled by a loud noise. Ergo, there is something which the baby hears and which startles it. Presumably "hearing sounds" is a kind of direct-object construction, to be explained away, and the explaining of explaining away comes later.)

To return to the slight and interesting differences. We, who are scribes, say of Agent that he believes that *Fb*. We conclude, therefore, case (1) (Subst.), that Agent believes that *Fc*. For we know (not necessarily that *b* even is *c*) but that Agent believes *b* is. Or perhaps we conclude, case (2) (E. G.), that there is someone whom Agent believes *F*'s, knwoing as we do that *b* really does exist. For the inference to be valid, Subst. requires that Scribe be able to add a premise asserting Agent's belief in an appropriate identity. For the inference to be valid, E. G. requires that Scribe be able to add a premise asserting the existence of the object of Agent's belief.

It is clear enough that the same patterns are exemplified in the perceptual ascriptions made by scribes of agents. (Since "see," for example, is so often linked with truth, we can resort to jargon and speak of "visual knowing" and "visual believing," this last perhaps amounting to believing that one visually knows. Generalizing across the sense modalities we can speak simply of sensuous knowing and believing.) To say that Agent sensuously believes that *Fb* entails that there is something which he sensuously believes to *F*, if the object of his perception exists. It is E. G., for belief or for perception, that is pertinent here. It will have been noticed that Hintikka's account of the nature of the premise whose addition reconstitutes the validity of E. G. is different, and stronger, than that given above. Hintikka requires not merely an added premise stating that the object of the agent's belief exists, but that the agent believes, truly, that it does so. Hintikka requires not merely that the object of the agent's sensuous belief exists, but (I think) that the agent *perceives who he is*. Are these stronger assumptions essential; i.e., do the weaker versions of E. G. sanction invalid inferences for the contexts of belief and perception? The answer is "no" on at least one transcription of these commonsense statements of belief or perception into a semantics close in spirit to Hintikka's own. If it is correct that Hintikka's stronger premises are not required to restore the validity of E. G., then the questions arise: Why does Hintikka plump for this stronger version? What implications does his choice have on other, and more philosophical, issues of perception? We try first to make plausible the claim that the weaker assumptions suffice to restore E. G. for ascriptions of belief or perception.

Scribes record agents' beliefs and perceptions. They need not of course do so in the agents' terms or using the agents' concepts or with the agents' beliefs. Scribes need not believe what agents do or share the same references. We distinguish, then, the beliefs and the singular terms belonging to Scribe from those belonging to Agent. Let "w^s" be the set of worlds compatible with what Scribe believes, and "w^a" the set compatible with what Agent believes. We need a predicate relativizing truths to worlds, and a predicate for keeping track of the membership of individuals in the worlds to which they belong. Let "T" be the former, and "B" the latter; "$Tw^a p$" is then shorthand for the assertion that the proposition p is true of the set of worlds compatible with what Agent believes. "$Bw^a c$" is shorthand for the assertion that the individual designated by "c" belongs to the set of worlds compatible with what a believes. We can now transcribe the mundane expression of an instance of E. G. from our Olympian vantage, employing rather natural assumptions about "truth-in-a-world," and making explicit to whom the references of terms belong. (See the "Addendum" to this paper for the transcription.) The central point in which the transcription differs from Hintikka's account resides in the fact that the transcription principles allocate the values of bound variables appearing in belief contexts to the worlds associated with their binding quantifiers. The result of the transcription turns out to be a theorem of standard, first-order logic.

Why then does Hintikka require the stronger premise that there exists someone whom the agent knows or believes, sensuously or not, to be identical with the object of his belief? It is not, I think, part of commonsense to do so. A youngster believes, perhaps, that Paul Bunyan has a big blue ox. We reject the conclusion that there is someone whom the youngster believes to have such an ox, not because the boy can't identify, or fails to know who this is, but because there is no such person. A freshman believes that Vercingetorix was dragged from his conqueror's chariot wheels —he's sure of the *tale*, but he isn't sure whether the tale is fact or fiction. *We*, it seems to me, correctly infer there really was someone whom the freshman believes to have been dragged, knowing (what he doubts) that Vercingetorix existed. This is to say that it is the existence of the required object, or the lack of it, but not the belief in the existence of the required object or lack of such beliefs, which makes these inferences valid or not. E.G. is in this way unlike, for instance, Subst., where the agent's belief and not the object's existence is the crucial thing.

Hintikka, it seems to me, is led to his stronger requirement because of a stronger, and I believe doubtful, principle about how quantifiers are to be understood. It is this principle which seems to determine later his treatment of direct-object constructions in perceptual contexts, and to underlie his introduction of a double set of quantifiers. In *Knowledge and Belief* (p. 155) Hintikka says of substitution instances of bound variables which appear in knowledge contexts that the agent must know to whom they refer; that universally quantified sentences of an agent's knowledge "are not naturally translated into ordinary language by a sentence beginning 'of each man a knows that'; we must rather use some locution like 'of each man known to a he knows that.' "

This principle of "relative agent omniscience" seems to me to be false, although we could easily add it to the semantics of belief so briefly sketched earlier. We need not tamper with the interpretation of the quantifiers to do so. To do so, we need add merely the "population assumption" that whatever a scribe refers to in speaking of an agent's beliefs inhabits the agent's worlds as well. Nonetheless, the principle seems to me to be pretty clearly unacceptable, for it precludes, or appears to preclude, our saying quite ordinary things. Take our freshman and Vercingetorix again. I want to say that there was someone, namely V., whom our freshman does not believe to have existed. But the natural symbolization of this, read back into English, comes out in Hintikka's translation to be that there was someone known to our freshman whom he believed not to exist. And this of course is not to be mistaken for the true (but irrelevant) statement that our freshman believes that someone, namely V., did not exist. The principle seems evidently false for it appears to preclude my saying that there exist objects of perception never sensuously known to Agent at all, and perhaps never physically known to him either. It appears to rule out the possibility of sensuously believing that something exists which one cannot identify, although perhaps discrimination, not identification, is all that Hintikka intends to require.

The need for which the principle of relative omniscience is introduced is not of course to provide that requisite objects exist. E.G., we have seen, comes through quite nicely with a simple existence assumption. The need which Hintikka feels is one we all share. We feel that to say that Agent believes thus-and-so is to say that he would, appropriately questioned, come out with the statement that thus-and-so. But then Agent must know about thus-and-so, and the objects referred to in saying this must thus be objects known to Agent. What we require, it seems, is not that quantifiers reaching into belief contexts be restricted in their range to objects known to Agent. For we can say significantly, often even truly, that there exist things which Agent does not know exist. We very often but not uniformly require, rather, that Agent believes there exists the object in question. If Agent believes that Fb, and if Agent believes that b exists, then Agent, like the rest of us, scribes and all, believes that something F's. Sometimes, however, Agent believes Fb, but doesn't believe b

exists. He does not then, for all we know, believe something F's, though something may exist and may be F ("*b*" perhaps is "Vercingetorix") or it may not ("*b*" perhaps is "Pegasus"). If Agent however does believe that b exists and that b F's, and if b does exist, then it follows that there is something which Agent believes to be identical with something which F's. The principle of relative agent omniscience seems far too strong to be true.

True or false, this principle seems to lie at the center of Hintikka's account of perception. It figures in the reduction of the direct-object construction to the propositional form. It appears to figure in laying sense-data to rest. The objects known to Agent may be known to him in different ways. For all of us there are physically distinct but perceptually indistinguishable entities, entities whose identification resides not in their appearance but, say, in their location. For most of us there are perceptually distinct but physically indistinguishable entities. Most of us allocate these perceptual differences to physically identical objects, speaking of perspective, or of their appearance from one place or another, and under one condition or another. Sense-data theorists presumably are a minority for whom perceptually distinct objects are thereby distinct objects. In any case, the point for Hintikka is that there are not two kinds of object, physical and perceptual, but one kind of object, which can be individuated both physically and perceptually. Since these objects are known to agents in distinct ways, the quantifiers, already restricted to range over the objects known to the agent (when prefixed to open sentences asserting his beliefs), now take on different senses. They differ as the objects known to the agent are physically or perceptually known to him. The sentences in which they occur will differ not only in the appearance of these distinct quantifiers but also in their concatenation with expressions of the agent's sensuous or nonsensuous beliefs.

Finally, Hintikka exploits the two types of quantifiers to give expression to direct-object constructions. He does so in a manner that makes their reduction to propositional ascriptions evident. Thus, we say that *Agent* sensuously *knows who* an object, b, is by saying that some object, *physically* known to Agent, is known by him to be identical with b; Agent perceives *who* b is. We say that *Agent perceives* b in saying that some object, *perceptually* known to Agent, is known by Agent to be identical with b; b is placed among the objects of Agent's perceptions; Agent *sees* b.

Since I argued earlier against the principle of "agent omni-science," I am committed now to rejecting Hintikka's double-quantifier theory, which, apparently, assumes that principle. On the other hand, any merit the earlier argument may have had we can borrow here. It would be nice, however, to muster additional doubts and further reasons for rejecting the double-quantifier theory. And, if that theory does fail, something needs to be said about direct-object constructions, and some account needs to be given of the differences in seeing who, seeing that, and seeing it.

Hintikka's account of the contrast between "seeing who" and "seeing it" is fairly swift. I am sure I am not in command of his double use of quantifiers and the distinctions they make available. One wonders why the quantifiers do, but proper names or pronouns or demonstratives do not (if they do not), bear the sense of the way in which the objects referred to by their use are known. In any case, with the two types of quantifiers, and with sensuous and nonsensuous belief operators, and with the occurrence of proper names by contrast with definite descriptions, we have eight distinct sentence types with which to express the way in which Agent knows an object. The number can, perhaps, be enlarged depending upon the manner in which the definite descriptions secure their uniqueness of reference. This, no doubt, attests to the subtlety with which nuances of commonsense assertions can be made formally explicit—and perhaps Hintikka will comment on these in helping us to understand his double-quantifier theory. Are we, for example, to distinguish "knowing Smith" and "know-ing who the president of First National is" as we have been in-structed in the distinction between "seeing Smith" and "seeing who the man in front of me is"? I suspect that the cases are not after all exactly parallel, and that what before was the characteri-zation of knowing who an object is, should, by symmetry with the perceptual case, now turn out to be simply : knowing the object. To say that there is an object, perceptually known to Agent, who Agent knows to be, say, president of First National, seems to say that Agent perceptually identifies the president, i.e., *recognizes* him. And to say that there is an object, physically known to Agent, who Agent knows to be Smith, seems to say, indeed, not merely that Agent knows Smith but who Smith is. Is it possible to say consistently that Agent sees something which he can't identify, i.e., which is not known to him? Apparently, it depends.

Read "perceptually individuate" for "identify," and the result appears to be a contradiction. To say that Agent sees something is just to say that Agent has perceptually individuated something. Read "identify" as "physically identify," and the conjunction of sentences of the form of Hintikka's (14) with the denial of his (7) is the apparently contingent result: there is something perceptually individuated by the agent but it is false that there is anything physically known to him with which it is identical. The sense of asymmetry between what is perceptually individuated and what is physically identified merely reflects, perhaps, the priority which physical identification maintains in determining the identity of objects. There are no obvious difficulties in principle raised by questions like these, only a nagging unclarity about details and applications which lie beyond the intended scope of Hintikka's paper.

More substantial, perhaps, are questions about the paraphrase of various types of grammatically direct-object constructions. Baby hears a sound. Good, then there is something which Baby hears. What is this? A sound? Are there then sense-data? Or are we to say that Baby hears something sounding, a rattle perhaps, but doesn't know—doesn't hear—that it is a rattle? Baby, perhaps, is at the stage of perceptual individuation but not physical identification. Nonetheless, *we* know that it is the rattle sounding, not sounds, which Baby hears. And to say that Baby hears a rattle is quite as simple a logical matter as saying that Agent sees Smith. It is to say that there is something, a certain rattle, which Baby hears although we have imagined the case in which Baby does not hear that it is a rattle. We know how to transcribe this last clause of ignorance into Hintikka's formal idiom. It is to say of the thing that Baby has perceptually individuated that there is nothing physically known to Baby with which Baby equates it. But how are we to transcribe the first clause? I am not at all sure. In blackboard English it comes to this: there is something perceptually individuated by Baby, which is a rattle, and which Baby hears, and perhaps this last means: which Baby hears to be something. In symbols using the perceptual quantifier we write: $(\exists x)$ (Baby hears that $(\exists y)$ $x = y$). So perhaps we *can* say that babies hear sounds, and even accept the inference that therefore there is something they hear. And perhaps we can accept all this without further premises and without appeal to sense-data. If so, we foresake now the pleasures of the crib for more adult pastimes.

John, drugged, hallucinates. He sees brightly colored objects which not only do not exist there, but do not exist. We all grant at once, sense-datum theorist and all, that it is false that there is something, physically known to John, which he sees in the specified way. But is it true that there is nothing which John sees? Can we say only that John sensuously believes that there is something fitting the specified description? Can we not say, given the resources of the double-quantifier theory, that there is something, perceptually individuated by John, which John sees to have certain properties, although there is nothing physically known to John with which it is identical? (Indeed, there is nothing physical at all with which it is identical.) This is to raise the sense-datum theorist's question, which turns on the sensuous nature of perception by contrast with nonsensuous belief, now reinforced by Hintikka's own distinction of types of quantifiers. For, although it is evident that one cannot infer from John's belief alone that there exists the object of his belief, can we not infer from John's perception alone that there exists *something* perceptually distinct, that we do see something, although not necessarily a physical thing? This of course would admit different ranges of values for the two types of quantifiers, and Hintikka denies that their ranges do so diverge. But isn't this exactly what is at issue? Why should we plump for Hintikka's account and not for the sense-datum theorist's? There is, on this latter view, something, perceptually individuated by John, for which there is no physically identifiable object with which it is identified. John sees this to be brightly colored in the required way. From the fact that John sees that the object before him is red, why should it not follow without further premise that there is something, perceptually known to John, which *is* red?

This is an unhappy consequence. It is a consequence we are not so likely to confront if we renounce the double-quantifier theory. For that theory appears to make it a matter of fact, not of logic, that a common set of objects comprises the set of what can be perceptually individuated by us and what can be physically identified by us. If this is a contingent matter, then the double-quantifier theory has no special purchase to bring to bear on sense-datum theories and the problems of perception.

It is of course equally not a matter of logic that determines what our standard quantifier ranges over. But the standard quantifier, without restriction to the objects of Agent's knowledge, sensuous or not, is apparently adequate to the distinctions Hintikka wishes to draw. And if it is, every consideration for simplicity of intellectual gadgetry, and every doubt about the principle of relative omniscience combine to support the attempt to express the semantics of perception with standard logic and special assumptions, but without special operators. It is one of the merits of Hintikka's treatment of the concepts of necessity and possibility in terms of model sets to have shown just how that can be done. How, then, are we to express with these resources the distinctions between perceiving an object, perceiving which one it is, and perceiving what it is? How are we to treat the various direct-object constructions of commonsense? And what, finally, is to be said of illusions and hallucinations?

To say that Agent sees something which exists is to say in blackboard English that there is something which Agent sensuously knows to be identical to something: (Ex) (a sensuously knows that (Ey) $(x = y)$). To say that Agent sees Smith who exists but doesn't know it is Smith is to say merely that Agent sees something which happens to be Smith: $(Ex)((x = s)$ & a sensuously knows that $(Ey)(x = y)$). To say that Agent sees Smith and knows it is Smith is to say there is something, Smith, such that Agent sensuously knows that it is identical to Smith: $(Ex)((x = s)$ & a sensuously knows that $x = s$).

Given the notions of an agent seeing something and of an agent seeing which thing it is, it is possible to give expression to judgments like: Agent sees something he can't identify, i.e., he sees something and he doesn't know which thing it is. It is possible to say that he sees something he doesn't believe exists, or that he thinks he sees something but doesn't, etc. And we have accordingly the basis for giving expression to what on the double-quantifier theory might have been described as a case of an agent seeing a perceptually individuated object which he cannot physically identify, or knowing which object a physically identifiable object is, but not perceptually individuating it on a given occasion.

We can say, then, that Baby hears a sound means that Baby hears something which sounds, granting that Baby can't identify what this is nor even know that this is. Similarly, I am inclined to believe that to say someone feels a pain is to say that the suffering individual is sensuously aware, painfully aware if you will, of a portion of his anatomy that hurts, although he cannot, perhaps, identify the portion and may not even know that this is the nature of the case.

We know, following Hintikka, how to give logical expression to the assertion that an agent sees a man, or that he sees Smith and moreover sees who he is. What are we to say of the agent who sees an object, say *b*, which does not exist? We can of course from our position as Scribe say that he thinks he sees something, but doesn't really; i.e., he sensuously believes there is something before him identical to *b*, that *b* is visually believed to exist, but doesn't in fact. We can of course say this, provided Agent believes that what he seems to see exists, but what if he does not believe this? Here, it seems, we need to borrow a notion from *Knowledge and Belief,* specifying that it is *possible, for all Agent sensuously knows,* that there is the required object before him. We add merely that, despite this, he doesn't believe there is.

This is not to pretend that we have a resolution of the features of hallucinatory experiences, say, which have led sense-datum theorists to posit nonphysical objects that we see. Like Hintikka, I believe that theory introduces illicit entities in an attempt to resolve genuine difficulties. Some of these difficulties are logical ones, resolved by an appropriate semantics and sensitive treatments, like his, of principles like E.G. and Subst. But not all of the difficulties are logical ones, and so not all of the difficulties are resolved by an enlarged semantics together with a restricted ontology. One of the difficulties is that we feel, when we record Agent as seeing, or seeming to see, what in fact does not exist, that there is nonetheless still something that he sees. He cannot, by hypothesis, photograph what he sees, but he can with words or paint show us a likeness of what he sees. There is then, it seems, something he sees which fits this likeness. From "Agent sees something" it follows that there is something which Agent sees. But if what he sees is not what it purports to be, what is it that he sees? The answer is not, I believe, that Agent sees sense-data, or images. The answer also is not, I believe, that the question is itself ill-begotten. But if the question is genuine, and if special, nonphysical, objects are not what we see, then it appears we must say that we see ordinary, and actual, physical objects even in cases of hallucination. And this, I believe, is the true answer. The answer is not required by the semantics of perception, though it is, of course, compatible with it. When the LSD user, peering at the sink, sees a satirical drain mouth with lidded, faucet eyes, he is seeing the sink. He is not seeing an actual grin, of course, but an actual sink, and sinks can look like that under conditions like those. What Agent sees then, always, is the actual world, or better, the physical items of the actual world. He sees them as having these qualities, and those properties, and as being disposed and distributed in various ways. Sometimes what Agent sensuously believes, and sometimes what is possible for all Agent sensuously knows, is incompatible with a true description of how things in fact physically are. We say then that Agent is seeing actual things as they actually aren't, and we have words for cases of these sorts, such as "illusion" and "hallucination."

Addendum: The semantical transcription of an instance
of E.G. for belief contexts.

For this we need to lay down certain principles governing the appearance and confinement of the truth or T-operator and introducing the world-membership or B-operator.

1. T-confinement.

$Tw^i\lambda pq \longleftrightarrow$ $\lambda\ Tw^ip\ Tw^iq$, where λ is any binary truth-functional operator.

$Tw^i\overline{p} \longleftrightarrow$ $\overline{Tw^ip}$, where '$\overline{p}$' is the negation of p.

$Tw^iExFx \longleftrightarrow$ $Ex\ \&\ Bw^ix\ Tw^iFx.$

$Tw^iKap \longleftrightarrow$ $\&\ Bw^ia\ Tw^ap$, where 'K' is some belief or perception operator.

$Tw^iFa \longleftrightarrow$ $\&\ Bw^ia\ Tw^iFa$, provided 'a' is a proper name which occurs within the scope of no belief or perception operator in 'F.'

We ignore here modal contexts expressing necessity or possibility. Various assumptions concerning iteration and such would give us various systems for distinguishing knowledge and belief and senses of these.

2. Using the T-confinement principles, we transcribe an ordinary instance of E.G., with the weak premise of existence, into its explicit semantical counterpart which ranges alongside. The

resulting transcription is an instance of an argument which matches a theorem of first-order logic. It proceeds in two steps: first, in relativizing the statements to the set of worlds compatible with what the scribe who lays down the argument believes; then, second, in applying the T-confinement principles to these.

Mundane argument	Relativization	Olympian transcription
1. $KaFb$	$Tw^{s}KaFb$	$\& Bw^{s}a \& Bw^{a}b \ Tw^{a}Fb$
2. $Ex \ x = b$	$Tw^{s}Ex \ x = b$	$Ex \& Bw^{s}x \& Bw^{s}b \ Tw^{s}x = b$
So $Ex \ KaFx$	$Tw^{s}Ex \ KaFx$	$Ex \& Bw^{s}x \& Bw^{s}a \& Bw^{a}x$ $Tw^{a}Fx$

Reply

JAAKKO HINTIKKA

Although there is an encouragingly large area of common ground between Professor Clark and myself, it is also obvious that some of the critical points he raises touch the central claims of my paper. It is therefore important to me to see what can be said about the questions he asks. This is important also because many of the doubts he voices are likely to occur to any reader of my paper. I am hence grateful to Professor Clark for having put forward these doubts as clearly and as reasonably as he has done, thus greatly facilitating the clarification of the issues involved.

If I were to express the main difference between my own line of thought and Professor Clark's, I would perhaps say that he is not radical enough. Among other things, he illustrates the peculiarities of the respective logics of perception and belief in terms of the contrast between an agent and a scribe and discusses the breakdown of existential generalizations (E.G.) largely in terms of the possible emptiness of the free singular term one is generalizing upon.[1] Both these lines of thought bring out certain relevant aspects of the situation, but they do not get to the bottom of the problem. We may have failures of the substitutivity of identity even when we are discussing our own beliefs or perceptions, although in this case the agent and the scribe coalesce. If I do not see whether the man in front of me is Mr. Smith or not, I cannot substitute "the man in front of me" for "Mr. Smith," even though the two happen to be one and the same person. To introduce an omniscient scribe looking above my shoulder is not to explain this failure of substitutivity. The basic feature of the logical situation seems to be the multiplicity of possible worlds, not their relativity to an observer.

[1]The latter feature of the situation seems to be taken by Clark to be a consequence of the former.

It is of course perfectly true that E.G. ordinarily fails when applied to an empty singular term. Professor Clark may be right in stressing this point, for it was intentionally neglected in my paper. However, elsewhere I have sought to analyze in some detail the problems thus caused.[2] The reason why I did not take up these problems in my paper is partly that they seem to have been solved in the nonmodal case, and that in the modal case they are in any case overshadowed by other, much more intriguing problems to which I restricted my attention.

These problems are not due to the failure of some free singular term to specify any existing individual but rather to their failure to specify a unique (well-defined) individual. These difficulties, so persuasively urged by Quine against our predecessors, still apply against Clark's own treatment of existential generalization, it seems to me. We can say that his proverbial freshman's beliefs about Vercingetorix are really about someone only because *we* know that Vercingetorix existed. This is (suitably understood) a *necessary* prerequisite of E.G., but it is not a *sufficient* one. It seems to me that Clark is smuggling in a tacit premise here concerning the freshman's knowledge (or beliefs). However firmly we know that Vercingetorix existed, if it should turn out that our freshman does not know who Vercingetorix was (perhaps the poor chap is apt to confuse him with the god Vervactor) nor have any clear opinions as to who he was, we could not say that there is any one individual of whom our freshman believes those things he has been told about Vercingetorix. Analogues to all the objections Quine has so eloquently elaborated against quantification into referentially opaque contexts can be used to the same effect here.

(Suppose you believe that the number of planets satisfies the equation $x^2 - 18x + 81 = 0$. Can I go ahead and conclude in virtue of E.G. that there is some number of which you believe that it satisfies this question? Only if you have some belief as to what number *is* the number of planets.)

The restriction which I have argued is needed here on the substitution values of bound variables is dubbed by Clark "the principle of relative agent omniscience." For reasons indicated, I cannot accept Clark's conclusion that this principle is "far too

[2]Principally in "On the Logic of Existence and Necessity," *The Monist,* 50 (1966), 55–76.

strong to be true." It seems to me that Clark, for all of his perceptiveness, has missed here an important part of the Quinean difficulties. In any case he does not seem to me to offer any full solution of the difficulties that have worried Quine and myself.

If one accepts these difficulties as genuine problems, and if one recognizes them as problems pertaining essentially to quantification into modal contexts, there is only one reasonable course left. This is precisely the restriction on the substitution values of bound variables which I have urged. This is shown (on certain very natural assumptions) in my recent paper "Individuals, Possible Worlds, and Epistemic Logic" for the concept of knowledge.[3] Other modal notions obviously follow suit.

Clark may be right in saying that the prerequisites I use are not "part of common sense." In view of the argument presented in the paper just mentioned, however, I venture to suggest that they are very much part of our common logic.

The prerequisite for the term *"a"* to be such a substitution value (say in the case of knowledge) is the truth of

(16)   "(Ex) b knows that $(x = a)$"

provided that we are merely discussing what b knows or does not know. The approximate meaning of (16) is colloquially expressed by "b knows who (or what) a is." The assumption that "the principle of relative agent omniscience" is redundant amounts to assuming that for every individual a', there is some term *"a,"* such that $a' = a$ and that b knows who or what a is. This, obviously, means assuming that every individual is known to each b under some suitable description or other. My restriction, which presupposes the denial of this assumption, is thus much more appropriately called the principle of relative agent *non*-omniscience than of relative agent omniscience. Clark's terminology here turns the facts (from my point of view) upside down.

Incidentally, Clark's term "agent omniscience" is also misleading for another reason. In the case of other propositional attitudes, we do not need assumptions of the form "(Ex) b knows that $(x = a)$" but analogous assumptions of the form "(Ex) b believes that $(x = a)$," "(Ex) b perceives that $(x = a)$," etc. Occasionally these different kinds of assumptions seem to be wrongly assimilated to each other by Clark (see the translation of (21) below). However, even in other respects, he would have to speak of relative agent omni-belief, relative agent omni-perception, etc., in addition to agent omniscience. It is possible, however, that Clark's confusion on this point is due to the excessive brevity and the lack of clarity of my own formulations.

It seems to me that there is a very natural explanation why Clark should underestimate the need for the principle of relative agent non-omniscience. This explanation turns on the distinction made toward the end of section III of my paper between statements about an individual and about whoever or whatever is referred to by a term. To see what this explanation is, let me quote Clark: "If Agent . . . does believe that b exists and that b F's, and if b does exist, then it follows that there is something which Agent believes to be identical with something which F's." If this is to be counted against my theory, it has to be construed as an inference from

(17) agent believes that $[(Ex)(x = b)$ & $F(b)]$ & $(Ex)(x = b)$

to

(18) $(Ex)(Ey)(x = y$ & agent believes that $F(y)$.

I have argued that this is a fallacious inference. However, Clark's inference is perfectly correct if its premise is construed as a statement, not about whoever b happens to be, but about the individual who in fact is b, as it in fact is naturally construed. Then it is an inference from

(19) $(Ey)[b = y$ & agent believes that $((Ex)(x = y)$ & $F(y))]$,

to (18). I suspect that this valid inference is what has inspired Clark's remark. However, on this interpretation, the validity of his inference cannot be used against my approach.

My suspicion that this is how some of Clark's key statements ought to be understood is reinforced by the fact that in other passages Clark is likewise presupposing a construction which in my terms turns his statement into a statement about "the individual who . . . ." For instance, we read: "To say that Agent sees Smith who exists but doesn't know [see?] it is Smith is to say merely that Agent sees something that happens to be Smith: $(Ex)((x = s)$ & a sensuously knows that $(Ey)(x = y))$."

As you can see, for all practical purposes this is my expression (15).

Incidentally, Clark's preoccupation with the existence presuppositions seems to have led him to misrepresent slightly the nature of the prerequisites which on my view are needed for a term to be a substitution value of bound variables in a modal context: "Hintikka requires not merely an added premise stating that the object of the agent's belief exists, but that the agent believes, truly, that it does so." The prerequisite attributed to me here is of the form

(20) a believes that $(Ex)(x = b)$

where b is the object of the agent's belief (i.e., a's belief). However, I do not want to impose *this* restriction, but rather require a premise of the form

(20)' (Ex) a believes that $(x = b)$,

which is not equivalent with (20). Clark continues: "Hintikka requires not merely that the object of the agent's sensuous belief exists, but (I think) that the agent perceives who he is." This is not altogether wrong, but it is not quite explicit. For the two different pairs of quantifiers, we need two different kinds of prerequisites. Only one of them is naturally rendered in our vernacular by speaking of the agent's *perceiving who* (say) b is. The other is (I have argued) expressed more naturally by speaking of the agent's *perceiving b* (direct-object construction). Clark's statement thus applies only to quantifiers relying on physical methods of cross-identification.

A similar distinction is needed in the case of knowledge (and belief). Since we normally rely on physical methods of individuation in using these concepts, the prerequisites have to be formulated almost always in terms of knowing who or what (or in terms of having an opinion of the identity of someone or something), *not* in terms of knowing someone or something (direct-object construction). The latter locution is appropriate only on the (relatively rare) occasions when individuation turns on the knower's personal situation. This fact necessitates an important qualification to the passage Clark quotes from p. 155 of my *Knowledge and Belief*. The parallelism between knowledge and perception which Clark expects to break down is vitiated only by the relative infrequency, unimportance, and imprecision of such personal methods of individuation.

The main specific objection Clark offers against my treatment of quantification into perceptual and other modal contexts is that "it precludes, or appears to preclude, our saying quite ordinary things." These ordinary things are exemplified by there being someone whom our freshman (call him Frosh) does not believe to have existed. But this is at once rendered in my symbolic jargon by

(21) $(Ex) \sim$ Frosh believes $(Ey)(y = x)$.

Clark says that if this is translated back into English, it comes out saying that there was something known to Frosh that he does not believe to have existed. For reasons indicated earlier, instead of "something known to Frosh" we have to speak here of someone of whose identity Frosh has an opinion. Apart from this, however, I do not see anything wrong in the re-translation. According to Clark, (21) was supposed to be true because Frosh had been told a number of things about Vercingetorix, whom he nevertheless does not think of as having actually existed. However, unless the things Frosh has been told about Vercingetorix, including his name, can be pinned on one particular ancient rather than on others, we cannot say of Vercingetorix that *he,* and no one else, is the man whose existence is disbelieved by Frosh. Frosh's tentative belief in these distinguishing characteristics is precisely what makes it true to say that he has an opinion of who Vercingetorix was (or might have been), and if this is not the case, there is nothing in Clark's example to justify the statement that there is some particular individual whose (past) existence is disbelieved by Frosh. Thus my symbolic formulation (21) does not contain any unnatural or foreign elements, but rather has the merit of spelling out an important tacit presupposition of our talk of individuals in a context where their existence is disbelieved by other people.

An apparent difficulty still remains, however, in that the counterpart of (21) for knowledge, i.e.,

(22) $(Ex) \sim$ Frosh knows that $(Ey)(y = x)$,

is inconsistent on the assumptions made in my *Knowledge and Belief.* This difficulty is only apparent, for I have repeatedly pointed out that it is merely due to a gratuitous minor assumption which I now find unacceptable for several reasons and which has nothing to do with the basis of my approach to quantification into modal contexts.[4] This is the assumption formalized by $(C.EK =)$ (and partly by $(C.EK =)^*$) to the effect that one can only *know who* someone is if one *knows that* he exists. If this assumption is given up, (22) will no longer be contradictory. No

[4] In addition to the *Noûs* paper mentioned in the preceding footnote, this point is made in my note, " 'Knowing Oneself' and Other Problems in Epistemic Logic," *Theoria,* 32 (1966), 1–13.

difficulty in my treatment of quantification into modal contexts is brought out by the fate of (22) in *Knowledge and Belief.*

In spite of this, giving up $(C.EK =)$ and $(C.EK =)^*$ and their analogues for other propositional attitudes may perhaps seem to lead to interpretational difficulties. The case of perception is as instructive as any. Here we may have truths of the form

(23) (Ex) b perceives that $(a = x)$,

although there is no actual individual who could be said to be the value of x which makes (23) true. The following would be a case in point: b hallucinates and sees a man in front of him. What is more, b clearly sees who this man is: it is his own father. But the father is long since dead, and hence cannot be a value of a quantifier ranging over ordinary physical individuals in the state of affairs. This possible truth of (23) in the absence of any ordinary physical individual who could serve as the appropriate value of x might perhaps be construed as an indication that I am after all committed to the existence of sense-data, for what else is there that could serve as the requisite values of x in (23)? Is my theory in the last analysis any better off than the old sense-datum theories?

Now I do not care greatly whether my theory is said to be committed to sense-data or not, as long as it is right. Nor do I think that sense-datum theories are necessarily wrong in all respects. However, I do think it is profoundly misleading to judge the commitment of a theory or of an analysis on the basis of one's first impressions of such symbolic expressions as (23). In general, such commitments can only be judged in terms of an explicit semantical theory but not on the basis of our feelings about this or that formula. In the present case, one is apt to be led astray by the usual glib talk of bound variables "ranging over" a set of entities. For reasons indicated in my paper, I do not find this idea helpful or even fully appropriate in modal contexts. In such a context, we are not given just one domain of individuals, but a number of such domains, one for each "possible world" we have to consider. Then questions of *unique* reference may become as important as questions of *nonempty* reference.

Many statements of Clark's are couched in terms of the "ranging over" locution. Accordingly, I find it very hard to tell whether these statements are really incompatible with what I maintain.[5]

---

[5]For instance, I do not think Clark is really arguing against me when he points out that the identity of the sets of values of the two kinds of

What happens in cases like (23) is nevertheless not particularly hard to understand in precise semantical terms. Here I can give only rough informal explanations. It is of course not true that questions of *unique* reference are always with us. When a bound variable occurs only outside modal operators, no comparisons between different possible worlds are involved, and the full import of the quantifier in question can be understood in terms of a bound variable which "ranges over" the individuals who exist in the actual world.

In the opposite extreme case, a bound variable may occur (as in (23)) solely within the scope of a modal operator. Then the question of actual reference becomes gratuitous, and the whole weight is placed on the uniqueness-of-reference requirement. This is precisely what happens in (23) and in comparable statements in terms of other propositional attitudes (or in terms of the other kind of quantifiers $(\exists x)$). Their force becomes one of an identification statement, devoid of existential import as far as the actual state of affairs is concerned.

In fact, even on intuitive terms this meaning of (23) is perfectly easy to grasp. The hallucinating agent b recognizes who the man in front of him is. This is a fact about his perceptions (apparent perceptions, if you want), which is naturally expressed by speaking of "perceiving who" or of "seeing who." If these locutions are to be translated into a reasonable symbolism the only candidate seems to be an expression like (23).

If you do not believe this, an argument from the parity of cases might help. If a exists, and if b's perceptions are correct, surely the appropriate translation of the locution "b perceives who a is" is (23). Now the phenomenological facts (b's impressions) can be the same no matter whether a exists in fact or not. Hence the same translation (23) ought to be used in all uses.

(If this argument smacks of a variant of the argument from illusion, it is not surprising, for I believe that we have here part of the true gist of this argument.)

---

quantifiers should not be a matter of contingent fact. Surely it is a matter of logic that any bound variable, in so far as it can in any sense be said to range over the actually existing objects, ranges in any case over the same objects.

Another case in point is Clark's formulation of my restriction on the substitution values of bound variables in modal contexts by speaking of a restriction on the range of these variables. Although this talk may have been encouraged by my own looser formulations, it is not fully explanatory.

Notice, incidentally, that the way *b* in our hallucination example identifies the man in front of him as his father is presumably by *physical* methods: by his looks, perhaps his way of speaking, etc. This fact (or assumption) is reflected by the presence in (23) of the quantifier (*Ex*), which relies on physical methods of individuation.

I hope that all this helps to dispel some of the surprise caused by the truth of (23). Nevertheless, you may still be puzzled by the presence of an existential quantifier in the symbolic transcript (23) of the "perceives who" locution when this is not supposed to carry a commitment to any actual existence. The full explanation of this use of an existential quantifier can only be given, it seems to me, by arguing that a quantification over certain objective entities is in any case implicit in our talk of "knowing who," "perceiving who," etc. This kind of argument is hinted at toward the end of my paper when the individuating functions are mentioned. I cannot elaborate it here, however, and hence have to rest my case on the explanations just given.

In conclusion, I wish to mention two smaller objections I have to Professor Clark's comments.

1. It seems to me obvious that, *pace* Clark's tentative suggestion, we cannot identify "visual belief" with "belief that one visually knows." In an illusion which the agent knows to be an illusion, we have a "visual belief" in one sense of the word: the world appears to the agent as if something were the case. However, he need not for this reason believe that the world is as it appears to be.

2. So far I have not discussed the phenomenological presuppositions of my approach, and it would take too long to do so here. Suffice it to say that I obviously have to assume that our spontaneous perceptions (perceptual beliefs) "come to us" already structured into individuals, their properties and relations etc., and not (say) as a two-dimensional continuum of color and shades. This presupposition seems to me satisfied, although I cannot argue for it here. Obviously, however, it may occasionally break down. Some of Clark's examples of what a baby hears seem to me to be cases in point. If so, they are simply marginal cases in which my analysis is not (in its present form) applicable.

This book is set in eleven-point Old Style No. 1. It was composed, printed, and bound by The Haddon Craftsmen, Inc., Scranton, Pennsylvania. The paper is Warren's Old Style, manufactured by the S. D. Warren Company, Boston. The design is by Mary Thomas and Edgar J. Frank.